Practi

CALI

1992

Hayit Publishing

[1st] Edition 1992
UK Edition: ISBN 1 874251 45 2
US Edition: ISBN 1 56634 000 4

© copyright 1992 UK Edition: Hayit Publishing GB, Ltd, London
   US Edition: Hayit Publishing USA, Inc., New York

© copyright 1991 original version: Hayit Verlag GmbH
   Cologne/Germany

Author: Ernst Helmus
Translation, Adaption, Revision: Scott Reznik
Print: Druckhaus Cramer, Greven/Germany
Photography: Volkmar E. Janicke, Caspar Franzen, Ernst Helmus,
United States Travel and Tourism Administration

All rights reserved   Printed in Germany

Using this Book

Books in the *Practical Travel* series offer a wealth of practical information. You will find the most important tips for your travels conveniently arranged in alphabetical order. Cross-references aid in orientation so that even entries which are not covered in depth, for instance "Holiday Apartments," lead you to the appropriate entry, in this case "Accommodation." Also thematically altered entries are also cross-referenced. For example under the heading "Medication," there appear the following references: "Medical Care," "Pharmacies," "Vaccinations."

With travel guides from the *Practical Travel* series the information is already available before you depart on your trip. Thus, you are already familiar with necessary travel documents and maps, even customs regulations. Travel within the country is made easier through comprehensive presentation of public transportation, car rentals in addition to the practical tips ranging from medical assistance to newspapers available in the country. The descriptions of cities are arranged alphabetically as well and include the most important facts about the particular city, its history and a summary of significant sights. In addition, these entries include a wealth of practical tips — from shopping, restaurants and accommodation to important local addresses. Background information does not come up short either. You will find interesting information about the people and their culture as well as the regional geography, history and current political and economic situation.

As a particular service to our readers, *Practical Travel* includes prices in hard currencies so that they might gain a more accurate impression of prices even in countries with high rates of inflation. Most prices quoted in this book have been converted to US$ and £.

Contents

Registry of Places

Anza Borrego Desert State Park	8
Barstow, Calico	10
Big Sur	12
Bodie	13
Carmel	17
Coastal State Highway 1/101	22
Columbia	22
Death Valley National Monument	27
Joshua Tree National Monument	39
Julian	40
Lake Tahoe	40
Lassen Volcanic National Park	44
Los Angeles	47
Mendocino	60
Monterey	61
Muir Woods National Monument	65
Napa Valley	65
Pacific Grove	69
Pismo Beach	71
Point Reyes National Seashore	72
Redwood National Park	76
San Diego	77
San Francisco	86
San Luis Obispo	102
San Simeon/Hearst Castle	102
Santa Barbara	104
Sequoia and Kings Canyon National Park	107
Seventeen Mile Drive	110
Solvang	113
Yosemite National Park	121

General Information

Accommodation	6
Alcoholic Beverages	7
Automobile Club	10
Bargaining	10
Beaches	12
Camping	15
Car Rental	16
Children	19
Climate	19
Clothing	22
Consulate	24
Crime	24
Cuisine	24
Culture	25
Customs Regulations	27
Discounts	31
Economy	32
Electricity	32
Entertainment	32
Geography	33
Health Insurance	35
History	35
Holidays and Celebrations	37
Hospitals	38
Insurance	38
Literature	46
Maps and Informational Materials	59
Medical Care	59
Money	61
Nature Reserves	66
People	70
Photography	71
Police	73
Politics	73
Postal System	74
Restaurants	77
Shopping	111
Sights	112
Speed Limits	113
Sports and Recreation	114
Telephones	115
Theft	115
Time of Day	115
Tourist Information	116
Tourist Season	117
Travel Documents	118
Travel in California	118
Travelling to California	120
Vegetation	121

Accommodation

There are numerous and good campsites for those travelling with a camping vehicle. If not travelling with a motor home or recreational vehicle, there are a number of accommodation options in various categories.

Hotels and **Motels** are usually comfortably furnished and at least equipped with air conditioning and a colour television. In almost every area, there will be a selection of accommodation in various categories. At many of these, a reservation is either required or recommended. Prices are calculated according to low and peak season and there are sometimes special rates like weekend specials. Prices for hotels begin at around $50 not including breakfast, whereas motels start for as little as $35. If a third person is travelling along, this lessens the average cost considerably since an additional person will usually pay only $5 to $8. Those who would like to travel as inexpensively as possible should ask for the price of the least expensive room. Lists of especially inexpensive motel chains are available by contacting the following addresses:

Budget Hotel Inns, P.O. Box 10656, 2601 Jacksboro Highway, Suite 202, Fort Worth, Texas 76114.

Days Inns of America, 2751 Buford Highway Northeast, Atlanta Georgia 30324.

E-Z 8 Motels, 2484 Hotel Circle Place, San Diego, California 92108.

Motel 6, 51 Hitchcock Way, Santa Barbara, California 93105.

Regal 8 Inn, P.O. Box 1268, Mount Vernon, Illinois 62864.

Thrifty Scot Motels, 1 Sunwood Drive, P.O. Box 399, Saint Cloud, Minnesota 56302.

Many of the motel chains offer toll-free 1-800 numbers for further information or to make reservations.

Howard Johnson: prices range between $65 and $100 depending on location. Wellesley Inns and Park Square Inns also belong to the Howard Johnson chain, charging about 30% less. Toll-free number: 1-800-654-2000.

Best Western: prices range from $40 to $90 depending on location. Toll-free number: 1-800-528-1234.

Econolodge: prices range from $40 to $70 depending on location. Toll-free number 1-800-446-6900.

Quality Inn: prices range from $50 to $75 depending on location. Toll-free number: 1-800-228-5151.

Ramada Inn: prices range from $70 to $150 depending on location. Toll-free number: 1-800-272-6232.

Bed & Breakfast: The network of bed & breakfast inns has meanwhile spread all across the United States; in California, there is an especially broad selection. Depending on the location and the distance of the bed & breakfast from principal attractions, prices for one night with breakfast range from $27 to $42.

The following addresses will be able to provide more information on prices and locations:

American Family Inn, 2185 A Union Street, San Francisco, California 94123; Tel: (415) 931-3083.

Digs West Bed & Breakfast Southern California, 8191 Crowley Circle, Buena Park, California 90621; Tel: (714) 739-1669.

Bed & Breakfast Santa Barbara, 4744 Third Street, Carpinteria, California 93103; Tel: (805) 684-3524.

Rent A Room International Southern California, 1032 Sea Lane, Corona Del Mar, California 92625; Tel: (714) 640-2330.

Youth Hostels: In many cities and towns, there are youth hostels charging from $6 to $12 per night, given that one presents a valid international youth hostel membership card. One should, therefore, obtain a membership card before departing for California.

Information is available through: American Youth Hostels, National Administrative Offices, 1332 I Street, North West, Suite 800, Washington DC 20005.

→Camping

Alcoholic Beverages

In California, alcoholic beverages may only be purchased by or served to persons over the age of 21. One litre of alcohol may be imported or transferred from another state.

→Cuisine

Animals and Wildlife →Nature Reserves

Anza Borrego Desert State Park

The town and oasis Borrego Springs, with a population of 1,400, lies at the heart of the Anza Borrego Desert State Park, approximately 76 miles northeast of San Diego. This desert park is one of the largest in the United States with an area of around 936 square miles. The park was named after the Spanish conqueror Juan Bautista de Anza, who marched through this land after departing from the Mexican city of Senora in 1755. "Borrego" means sheep in Spanish. This park is especially worth visiting during the spring when countless blossoming plants paint the valley. In summer, the average temperatures of 94 to 108 °F in the shade scare off most tourists.
→Julian

Anza Borrego Desert State Park / Selected Sights and Hiking Areas

Blair Valley: In Anza Borrego Desert State Park, a number of cliff paintings point to the earlier history of the region, which archaeologists can trace back 12,000 years. The first inhabitants were the Cahuilla and Diegueno. The one mile long Pictograph Trail in Blair Valley leads to some of these cliff paintings, whose meaning is still not completely understood. The hike is also made attractive by the various types of cactus — the agaves, yuccas and catalpas.

Borrego Palm Canyon: Not far from the visitors centre, Palm Canyon is one of the most beautiful areas in this state park. A hiking path measuring about four miles connects four different oases with each other, in which over 700 palms can be found. With a little luck, one might be able to spot a big horn sheep here. The trail begins at the Borrego Palm Canyon Campsite.

The most popular trail in this desert park is about 3¼ miles (there and back) in length. The Borrego Palm Canyon Nature Trail leads to a picturesque oasis.

Tamarisk Grove: Quite near to the S 3 and State Road 78, two short and easy hiking paths begin at the Tamarisk Grove Campsite. Cactus Loop Trail is the first, about ½ mile long, leading in a circuit by a number of different species of cactus. This trail is especially impressive during the spring when the cactus plants are in full bloom. The other trail leads to the Yaqui Well, a spring which attracts many desert animals — foxes, lynxes, coyotes, deer and a number of aquatic birds.

When hiking, one should be sure to note certain facts.

One needs $3^{1}/_{2}$ quarts of water per day in this area where the temperatures can exceed 123 °F.

Wear stable shoes and a hat.

Never hike alone and inform friends or the park administration of planned hiking routes.

The visitors centre is open daily from 9 am to 5 pm from the beginning of October to the end of May and from the beginning of June to the end of September, Saturdays and Sundays from 10 am to 3 pm. Park Information: Tel: (619) 767-4684.

Anza Borrego Desert State Park / Practical Information

Accommodation

Camping: Borrego Palm Canyon, 117 tent and RV sites $14 to $22, located about two miles west of Borrego Springs.

Tamarisk Grove, 27 tent and RV sites (maximum length 21 feet), $14, 12 miles south of Borrego Springs between the road number 78 and S 3.

Bow Willow, 16 tent and RV sites, simply equipped, $10, 52 miles from Borrego Springs on the S 2.

The following very simply equipped campsites can be used free of charge. Their location can be inquired at the visitor center: Culp Valley, Yaqui Pass, Yaqui Well, Sheep Canyon, Arroyo Salado, Blair Valley, Fish Creek, Mount Palm Springs (listed according to their distance from the park headquarters in Borrego Springs).

Hotel: La Casa del Zorro, 3845 Yaqui Pass Road, P.O. Box 127, Borrego Springs, CA 92004, from $50 in summer and from $100 for one and two guests in spring and autumn, an additional person is charged $10. Tel: (619) 767-5323 or (in California) 1-800-824-1884, (in the US) 1-800-325-8274.

Motels: Oasis Motel, 366 Palm Canyon Drive, $35 to $40 for one and two persons, an additional person costs $5, Tel: (619) 767-5409. Stanlund's Motel, 2771 Borrego Springs Road, $45 to $70 for one and two persons, additional person $5, Tel: (619) 767-5501.

Reservations are recommended in the hotel and the two motels especially from October to May. Address: Borrego Springs Chamber of Commerce Desert State Park, P.O. Box 66, Borrego Springs, CA 92004, Tel: (619) 767-5555.

Emergency: The emergency telephone number for ambulances, the police and fire department is 911.

Medical Care: On the S 3 near the La Casa Del Zorro hotel complex is the Scripps Medical Clinic.

Important Addresses

Park Headquarters: Anza Borrego Desert State Park. P.O. Box 428, Borrego Springs, CA 92004, Tel: (619) 767-5311.

Automobile Club

The American Automobile Association is a partner organisation with a number of other national automobile associations throughout the world. If coming to California from a foreign country, often membership in foreign associations entitles members to automatic membership in the "triple A." Those travelling by car should definitely note the 24-hour emergency number, Tel: 1-800-336-HELP.

Bargaining

In California, like everywhere in the United States, prices are generally set. It can, however, be the case when purchasing more expensive items like camera equipment that one can bargain with the price. If planning a trip to Mexico, the opposite is the case. In Tijuana, for example, it is expected that the buyer will bargain with the price. This is also true for peddlers or Indians selling handicrafts.

Barstow, Calico

Beginning in the 19th century, this city in the Mojave Desert was very significant due to the mining industry. Today, the 20,000 residents live from, on the one hand, the various military facilities in the city and on the other hand, from tourism. Tourists are attracted to the region by the ghost town of Calico located 11¼ miles away. The deserted city of Calico provided over 2,500 prospectors with their livelihood between 1881 and 1896 when silver was found in the surrounding mountains. Today, experts estimate the value of the silver mined during that period at over 13 million dollars. When the price for silver sank drastically in 1895, the prospectors quickly abandoned the mines and moved on, in search of a new livelihood. The city of Calico died out, decayed and blossomed once more less than 100 years later as a tourist attraction.

The visitors not only come for a peek into the "wild 80's" of the past century, visitors can actually take part in the happenings. After having found a parking place ($3), the Playhouse Theatre charges $1.75 for admission. A tour of a mine, a wooden shed as well as a ride in an Old West train cost $1.75 per attraction, while one can play cowboy at the shooting gallery for $1. Admission to the museum is free of charge, offering an impression of earlier life in this city. It is open daily from 9 am to 5 pm.

The marketing of this ghost town as a tourist attraction does colour the raw reality of the years 1881 to 1896 substantially. A more realistic understanding of this time can be found, for example, in →*Bodie*.

Barstow, Calico / Practical Information

Accommodation

Camping: Barstow/Calico KOA, 74 tent and RV sites, $15-20 for two persons, additional person $2.50, 35250 Outer Highway 15 North, reservations are recommended, Tel: 1-800-KOA-0059 and (619) 254-2311.

Calico Ghost Town Regional Park, 114 tent and RV sites, $10 per site, located on Ghost Town Road, Tel: (619) 254-2122.

Motels: Barstow Inn, 1261 East Main Street, $35 to $55 for one and two persons, an additional person $4, Tel: (619) 256-7581.

Stardust Inn, 901 East Main Street, $35 to $55 for one and two persons, additional person $4, reservations are recommended, Tel: (619) 256-7116.

Sunset Inn, 1350 West Main Street, $35 to $55, one and two persons, additional person $5, reservations are recommended, Tel: (619) 256-8921.

Information: The Barstow Way Station Visitor Centre at 831 Barstow Road offers, in addition to the information desk, an interesting exhibition on the living conditions in the Mojave Desert. Tel: (619) 256-3591. Calico Museum, Tel: (619) 254-2122.

Restaurants: Steak-Eater's Inn, 1050 East Main Street, sometimes with live entertainment, reservations are recommended, Tel: (619) 256-2334.

Beaches

The most beautiful beaches for swimming, surfing and the like are located between San Francisco and San Diego. Along this section of coastline, there are mainly gently sloping beaches and even some beautiful coves. This, with the exception of Big Sur with its impressive and rugged coastal cliffs. The farther south one travels, the longer, wider and flatter the beaches become. The water temperature increases gradually the farther south one goes.

Big Sur

This entire coastal region, with the Santa Lucia Range to one side and the rocky Pacific coastline on the other, extends for a total of 65 miles and is one of the most beautiful sections of Highway 1 between San Francisco and Los Angeles. This region, part of which is still covered with the native vegetation, combines thick forests with redwood groves, a few lighthouses, and secluded, hardly accessible coves with the magnificent coastal cliffs. Henry Miller, who lived along this section of the coast from 1947 to 1964, wrote the following about Big Sur: "... a region in which one is aware of the weather, the space and the greatness of the landscape's eloquent silence."

A special attraction within this region is the Pfeiffer Big Sur State Park with the beautiful redwoods along the Big Sur River. In summer, the park rangers offer an informative nature programme.

Information: Tel: (408) 667-2315.

Big Sur / Practical Information
Accommodation
Camping: Big Sur Campground, on Highway 1, 2 miles north of Pfeiffer Big Sur State Park, 90 tent and RV sites, camping under redwood trees, from $16 for two persons, additional person $3, reservations are recommended, Tel: (408) 667-2322.

Riverside Campground, not far from Big Sur campground on Highway 1, 40 tent and RV sites, from $16 for two persons, additional person $3, reservations are recommended, Tel: (408) 667-2414.

Pfeiffer Big Sur State Park Campground, 217 tent and RV sites, maximum length of RV's is 27 feet, $10 per site, Tel: (408) 667-2315.

Motels: Big Sur Lodge, one and two persons from $65 to $100, additional person $5 to $10, on Highway 1 in the Pfeiffer Big Sur State Park, reservations are recommended, Tel: (408) 667-2171.

Ventana Big Sur, one and two persons from $130, additional person $25, exclusive hotel on an elevation with a view of the Pacific Ocean, 29 miles south of Carmel, approximately 1/2 mile from the turn-off from Highway 1, follow the signs, reservations are recommended, Tel: (408) 667-2331.

Restaurants: Glen Oaks Restaurant, on Highway 1, 1 1/4 miles north of Pfeiffer Big Sur State Park, a good restaurant, especially for fish, reservations are recommended, Tel: (408) 667-2623.

Bodie

The name of this town can be traced back to S. Body or William S. Bodie, who discovered gold in 1859 here. During the subsequent years, the mines could support only a few prospectors. However, with the spread of rumours of gold, the location of Bodie was divulged and this small settlement experienced an explosion in its population. During its "golden age" (1879-1881), Bodie was home to over 10,000 distrustful adventurers. It had the reputation of being the most wild and lawless gold mining towns in the west. Murders, robberies and street brawls were on the daily agenda. The unhealthy level of lead in the air on the streets of Bodie made for a relatively short life expectancy.

Today, Bodie lies peacefully and abandoned 20 miles southeast of Bridgeport amid a barren landscape. Bodie is a ghost town. Driving over the, in part, poor roads to Bodie is definitely worth the effort. About 170 wooden buildings have been preserved and offer a good impression of what life might have been like, although these preserved buildings make up only five percent of the entire city. In the small salons, there are still old furnishings, newspapers, articles of clothing, kitchen utensils, toys and much more under a thick layer of dust. The houses seem to have remained untouched since the time when they were hastily abandoned. The town is only now being protected from further decay.

The small wooden Methodist Church is still in quite good condition as are some of the saloons, the building housing the presumably successful and affluent undertaker, the school, the store and the Standard Company's mines in the eastern part of Bodie. It is estimated that 30 companies earned a total of $100 million during Bodie's heyday.

This ghost town was declared a state historic park in 1962, charging an admission fee of $3 per vehicle. The road to Bodie branches off of US 395 between Lee Vining on Mono Lake and Bridgeport. It is best to take State Road 270 rather than the 167 because it is in better condition with only 3 miles of unpaved road in poor condition, in comparison to the 11¼ miles when taking 167. However, during the winter months, both routes are usually impassable.

The former prospecting town of Bodie; now a ghost town

The park is open all year, in summer from 9 am to 7 pm, otherwise from 9 am to 4 pm.

Information: Bodie State Historic Park, P.O. Box 515, Bridgeport California 93517; Tel: (619) 647-6445.

Camping

Those who chose to camp while travelling through California will quickly learn the difference between public and private campsites. Public campsites can be found in all of the national parks and most of the state parks. These differ from private campsites in that the fees for use are much lower and are equipped more simply. Some very modestly equipped campsites can be used free of charge, others charge a fee between $4 to $9 per tent site. As a rule, all publicly run campsites operate on a first come first serve basis, making it necessary to arrive early enough to find a vacant spot.

Reservations can only be made at the larger campsites and well known national parks like Yosemite, Sequoia and King's Canyon National Parks, as well as at Joshua Tree National Monument.

Only reservations in writing or made in person are accepted. This can also be arranged through the Ticketron Agencies in Los Angeles, Broadway Department Store, 7th Street, and in San Francisco, Downtown Center Box Office, 325 Mason Street.

Reservations in writing can be made up to eight weeks in advance by contacting: Ticketron, Department R, 401 Hackensack Avenue, Hackensack, New Jersey 07601 USA.

The private campsites, in contrast, have every amenity imaginable: washing machines, dryers, electrical hook-ups, swimming pools etc. The prices for these range from $10 to $20 for two persons per night; an additional person will pay between $1 and $4. The fees in trailer parks which are mainly for RV's can be up to $30 per night.

Reservations are accepted at all private campsites and are even required by some.

Information on State Campsites

State Parks
Department of Parks and Recreation
P.O. Box 942896
Sacramento, CA 94296-0838
Tel: (916) 445-6477

National Parks and Forests
U.S. Forest Service
Appraiser's Building
630 Sansome Street
San Francisco, CA 94111

Western Regional Information Office
National Park Service
Fort Mason Building 201
San Francisco, CA 94123
Tel: (415) 556-4122 or (415) 556-0560

National Park Service Information Centre
Santa Monica Mountains National Recreation Area
22900 Ventura Boulevard
Suite 140
Woodland Hills, CA 91364
Tel: (818) 888-3440 or (818) 888-3770

Information on Private Campsites
California Travel Parks Association
P.O. Box 5648
Auburn, CA 95604
Tel: (916) 885-1624

Car Rental

Branch offices of the larger rental agencies like Avis, Hertz, National, Budget, Alamo etc., can be found at every airport and in larger cities and towns. Interesting for foreign visitors is that these grant discounted prices when a rental car is booked from a foreign country. Such bookings can be made through automobile clubs and travel agencies.

In addition to the large agencies, there are also smaller firms, which rent out their vehicles for as little as $15 per day including tax and insurance. These firms will be listed in the local yellow pages. Often, one can get good tips in hotels, motels, at campsites and service stations. The rental vehicles from smaller firms, however, often must be returned where they were rented, whereas the larger companies allow customers to return the vehicle at any given city.

One should note the following when renting a car:

- The mandatory insurance is often not sufficient; one should therefore opt for the supplemental insurance package for about $8 per day.
- The renter must be at least 21 years of age at most rental companies.
- The renter must hold a valid driving licence. For foreign visitors, a national driving licence is sufficient, but and international driving licence could speed up the process.
- Many firms will only accept the deposit for the vehicle in the form of a credit card.
- Many rental agencies do not allow the vehicles to be taken into Mexico or Death Valley.
- It is difficult to state exact prices because these vary from city to city. As a general rule, one should plan to spend around $150 per week on a rental vehicle.
- Those interested in especially inexpensive fares should look into the "Rent a Wreck" selection. These vehicles are a few years old, but fulfil their purpose.

→ *Insurance*

Carmel

The town of Carmel (population 5,000) was founded in 1888 on the Monterey peninsula. Carmel offers an interesting mixture of Mediterranean flair and American bustle. A stroll through the pretty and unusual shops and galleries is most definitely worth mentioning.

The mission of San Carlos Borromeo de Rio Carmelo — Carmel Mission for short — on Rio Road was founded by Serra on the Monterey Bay on June 3, 1770 and then moved to its present location in Carmel on August 24, 1771. This remained Serra's residence until his death in 1784, becoming his final resting place. The grave is in front of the alter in this old mission church. A tour through the mission is reminiscent of a visit to a museum due to the many old objects and documents from the founding years on display. Hardly any other mission in California has so much to tell in regard to its own development as well as the development of the region in general. The mission can be visited Monday to Saturday from 9:30 am to 4:30 pm and Sundays from 10:30 am to 4:30 pm. Admission is free of charge, Tel: (408) 624-3600.

Carmel / Practical Information
Accommodation
Camping: Carmel Valley Riverside RV Park, about 3½ miles on Carmel Valley Road after the turn-off from Highway 1 then 1¼ miles on Schulte Road, 35 RV sites, no tents, from $20 for two persons, each additional person $2, reservations are recommended, Tel: (408) 624-9329.

The mission in Carmel is the last resting place of its founder Pater Serra

Motels: Carmel River Inn, near the Carmel River Bridge, from $50 for two person, additional persons $5 each, reservations are recommended, Tel: (408) 624-1575.

Carmel Wayfarer Inn, 4th Avenue and Mission Street, $55 to $100 for two persons, additional persons $10 each, reservations are recommended, Tel: (408) 624-2711.

Restaurants

Anton & Michel, Ocean and Seventh Street, good restaurant, reservations are recommended, Tel: (408) 624-2406.

Clam Box Restaurant, on Mission Street between 5th and 6th Avenue, serving mainly fish dishes, Tel: (408) 624-8597.

Fish House on the Park, 6th Avenue and Junipero Street, fish specialities, reservations are recommended, Tel: (408) 625-1766.

Checks →*Money*

Children

In many regards, California is not only a paradise for adults, but holds a very special attraction for children. In the amusement parks of Disneyland and Knott's Berry Farm in Los Angeles and Sea World and the San Diego Zoo in San Diego, there is much to see, experience and take part in for children and adults alike. There are a number of tour agencies in the larger cities which offer tours especially for children. The services offered include everything from tours to parties to baby sitting and day care. Further information is available through the tourist information centers or in the yellow pages of the local telephone book.

Almost all of the admission prices are discounted for children *(→Discounts)*.

Climate

California's geographical location between the Sierra Nevadas and the Pacific makes for a mild coastal climate. Owing to the Pacific currents coming from the west, there is not that much difference in the summer and winter temperatures. It is more appropriate to refer to a rainy season (winter) and a dry season (summer).

While the southern regions of California have rain only seldom and have warm to hot temperatures, one will encounter sudden rain showers and cooler temperatures in the northern regions. Along the coast, there is often fog in the early morning hours, especially during the last four months of the year, while inland, in the extensive desert regions of southeastern California, visitors will encounter temperatures over 105 °F (40 °C) and it is not uncommon that temperatures will reach 123 °F (50 °C).

Highest, Lowest and Average Temperatures in °F (°C)

Sacramento

	High	Low	Average
January	54 (12)	39 (4)	46.5 (8)
February	59 (15)	43 (6)	46.5 (8)
March	65 (18)	45 (7)	56 (13)
April	72 (22)	46.5 (8)	56 (13)
May	79 (26)	52 (11)	68 (20)
June	88 (31)	56 (13)	68 (20)
July	96 (35)	59 (15)	76 (24)
August	90 (32)	58 (14)	76 (24)
September	90 (32)	58 (14)	68 (20)
October	79 (26)	52 (10)	68 (20)
November	65 (18)	45 (7)	48 (9)
December	56 (13)	39 (4)	48 (9)

Los Angeles

	High	Low	Average
January	65 (18)	46.5 (8)	58 (14)
February	66.5 (19)	48 (9)	58 (14)
March	68 (20)	50 (10)	61 (16)
April	70 (21)	54 (12)	61 (16)
May	74 (23)	56 (13)	66.5 (19)
June	77 (25)	59 (15)	66.5 (19)
July	83 (28)	63 (17)	74 (23)
August	83 (28)	61 (16)	74 (23)
September	83 (28)	61 (16)	72 (22)

October	77 (25)	58 (14)	72 (22)
November	74 (23)	52 (11)	61 (16)
December	68 (20)	48 (9)	61 (16)

San Francisco

	High	Low	Average
January	56 (13)	43 (6)	52 (11)
February	58 (14)	43 (6)	52 (11)
March	63 (17)	45 (7)	54 (12)
April	63 (17)	46.5 (8)	54 (12)
May	66.5 (19)	58 (14)	58 (14)
June	70 (21)	52 (11)	58 (14)
July	72 (22)	54 (12)	59 (15)
August	72 (22)	54 (12)	59 (15)
September	74 (23)	54 (12)	63 (17)
October	70 (21)	52 (10)	63 (17)
November	65 (18)	46.5 (8)	54 (12)
December	58 (14)	43 (6)	54 (12)

San Diego

	High	Low	Average
January	65 (18)	43 (6)	56 (13)
February	65 (18)	48 (9)	56 (13)
March	66.5 (19)	52 (10)	59 (15)
April	66.5 (19)	54 (12)	59 (15)
May	68 (20)	58 (14)	63 (17)
June	70 (21)	59 (15)	63 (17)
July	76 (24)	63 (17)	70 (21)
August	77 (25)	65 (18)	70 (21)
September	77 (25)	63 (17)	68 (20)
October	74 (23)	59 (15)	68 (20)
November	70 (21)	52 (10)	59 (15)
December	66.5 (19)	46.5 (8)	59 (15)

Clothing

California is considered a travel destination throughout the entire year (→*Climate*). It is, therefore, a good idea to take light and comfortable clothing although one should also pack a warm sweater. Along the coast in the northern regions of California, it can get quite chilly, especially in the mornings and evenings. A definite must are comfortable walking shoes which can withstand an occasional hiking tour — this because of the many national parks and the cities which are best explored on foot.

Coastal State Highway 1/101

US Highway 101 extends along the Pacific coastline from Mexico all the way to the northern extremes of the state of Washington. This is considered one of the most beautiful stretches of roadways in the United States. Within California, it is foremost a motorway, because it is surpassed in beauty by far by State Highway 1, which branches off from Highway 101 in Leggett. State Highway 1 runs parallel to the coast through San Francisco and Los Angeles to San Clemente.

Driving on this roadway alone makes a visit to California worth the trip. One should definitely make frequent stops to marvel at the breathtaking views of the steep coastal cliffs and the secluded bays. One drives through impressive redwood groves, small fishing villages and historical cities — and, especially in the south, the lively beach resorts.

Columbia

Columbia is, like Jamestown and Angles Camp among others, a town which one will come upon when travelling down the State Road 49. Like the others it originates from the gold rush era and makes the effort to keep this heritage alive.

Columbia's well preserved and restored mining town has meanwhile become a heavily visited State Historic Park. That which can be seen here includes the old gold washing equipment, a schoolhouse, a dentist's office, a drug store, saloons, a jail, the newspaper office, the Wells Fargo Express building and much more from the times of shiny gold nuggets and dull lead bullets.

Almost all of the buildings have old furnishings and the original equipment which is made more accessible to the visitor through music, picture presentations and figures which completes the scenes from this time. There is a museum with a slide show pertaining to the gold rush era. In Columbia, this was from 1850 to 1880.

Columbia / Practical Information
Accommodation
Camping: Marble Quarry Resort, 11551 Yankee Hill Road, 25 sites for tents, 22 sites for RV's, all hook-ups for motor homes etc., laundry facilities, swimming pool, tow persons from $16 to $20, each additional person $3, reservations are required during the peak season, Tel: (209) 532-9539.
Motels: Columbia Gem Motel, on Columbia Highway from about 1 mile from the State Historic Park, from $25 to $35 for one person, $30 to $60

Visitors should definitely plan a few days into their travel initerary to explore the coastal highway between San Francisco and Los Angeles

for two persons depending on the season, additional person $3, reservations are required during peak season, Tel: (209) 532-4508.

Theatre: The Fallon Theater takes on the role of a cultural centre with performances from the middle of June to the middle of August.

Performances: adults $10, children under 13, $7 to $10.

Information and Reservations: Tel: (209) 532-4644; during the off season, Tel: (209) 446-2116.

Consulate

British Consulate
3701 Wilshire Boulevard
Los Angeles, California
Tel: (213) 385-7381

Credit Cards →*Money*

Crime

Despite sensational news articles about the Californian metropolitan areas in the national and international press, crime should not hinder a pleasant visit to California. Tourists can do their part in lowering the crime rate by not flaunting valuables and avoiding the "less safe" areas of town during the late evening hours. In an emergency one should dial 911 for immediate assistance or dial the operator (0).
→*Theft*

Cuisine

The food in California is a reflection of the ethnic diversity of its residents (→*People*) and the "Californian culture." In almost every city there are Chinese, Japanese, Mexican and Italian restaurants, serving good and reasonable priced food. Depending on the region one can also find Korean, Cuban, Puerto Rican, Persian, Indian, Indonesian, German and French cuisine.

California is world famous for the variety and quality of its seafood. Shrimp, crab, lobster, shellfish and every imaginable variety of fish is available in innumerable restaurants, especially along the coast.

Culture

When describing the culture of California, one must take into account the various influences that have shaped the culture of California.

First of all is the cultural influence of and cultural legacy of the Spanish and Mexican conquerors, which is especially obvious through the Spanish Franciscan missions, the remnants of a culture which influences the architecture in California even today. One will without question come upon traces of this culture from San Diego north to San Francisco, whereby the influence is stronger in the southern regions of the state. Some of the Californian cities have a preserved historical core, dating back to the Spanish and Mexican era. Some cities have even mapped out walking tours of the city, allowing better understanding of this past, for example in Monterey. In some regions of California, the historical background plays a subordinate role to commercial interests, making discovering the true history of a city only possible with a great deal of effort. The simple, practical and beautiful architecture influenced by California's Mexican and Spanish era is experiencing a renaissance, especially in the southern regions.

In the middle of the 19th century, the frenzy of the gold rush was the major influence on California's cultural profile. Anglo-Americans and Europeans flocked to the "golden state" during this period. The cultural upheaval which ensued would undermine the existing Hispanic influences and establish a new lifestyle based on ideals like an enterprising pioneer spirit and progress. In addition, there was the wish for the classical past of Europe to take root and be preserved in California. This influence begins in the Mother Load Country and continues to Hearst Castle, the pompous residence of the newspaper magnate Randolph Hearst near San Simeon and the various museums in the larger metropolitan areas along the coast, ending in Silicon Valley near Palo Alto.

On a completely different level, the Asian culture played a significant role in the cultural development of California. The Asians not only influence entire districts of cities (Chinatown, Japantown) in San Francisco and Los Angeles (New Chinatown and Little Tokyo), but draw attention to their culture through a number of notable collections in well known museums like in the Asian Art Museum, a part of the De Young Memorial Museum in San Francisco. The dominating culture of California in the twentieth century, however, is influenced by the film industry. This is true all over the United States and all over the world for that matter, but nowhere is it so apparent as in California, home to Hollywood and near the show center of Las Vegas.

Many readers might ask themselves what has become of the influence of the Native Americans on the culture of California. In the California of today, this influence is hardly noticeable. However, those who seek will find, especially in some of the national parks like Yosemite, where the Native American culture is still alive.

On the one side, the present-day culture of California seems to be a reflection of the cultural diversity of the state's past; on the other side, it is characterised by a "trend-setting." It seems that California is forerunner in setting trends that sweep the western culture: ten-speed bicycles, skateboards, roller skates — even the surfing trend, which started in

The American culture on a building fasade — Benny Goodman & Co.

Hawaii, was brought to the status of lifestyle of an entire generation in California. Baseball jackets, Bermuda shorts, cycling shorts — not all of the fashion trends come out of Paris or Milan — are Californian trends, where question of historical origin is of little interest.

To bring a culture — namely the culture of California — into one composite picture is a difficult task, when one considers the size and incredible diversity of this state. But perhaps it is this inability to summarise "the" Californian culture which describes it best.

Customs Regulations

For those arriving in California from countries other than the United States, it is important to note the following: before landing, a customs form must be filled out. This is an official declaration that one is bringing no more than 200 cigarettes or 50 cigars, one litre of alcoholic beverages and that the value of gifts brought along does not exceed $100.

At the Californian borders, officials will check all produce, plants and animals before allowing entrance to California. A quarantine or confiscation is possible. Pets over four months must have certification of rabies vaccination administered within the past year.

Death Valley National Monument

Death Valley is known as "the most beautiful desert in the world," covering an area of 3,089 square miles. It is almost 126 miles in length with a width of only 4 to 16 miles. The ominous name of this landscape dates back to the winter of 1849, when pioneers attempted to cross this valley in the belief that they had found a shortcut to the gold mines in the west. The lack of food and water transformed these people in to a brawling hoard. Each of them tried to finally get out of the hideous desert; most died before achieving this.

Later, the surprising discovery of Borax aroused new interest in this valley. The early miners built roads to transport the loads, often weighing more than 36 metric tons, using the famous twenty-mule teams. One and a quarter miles north of the Furnace Creek Oasis, the Harmony Borax Interpretive Trail leads to a small factory, which was the first to successfully process Borax in 1883.

Today, this valley with the foreboding name has advanced to the status of tourist attraction. Those who visit this valley will always notice a slight distortion in the clear air over the dried out earth, due to the ascending heat. The sky is perpetually blue. Six months of the year, there is relentless heat; in the remaining months, the sun loosens its grip only slightly. The desert has diverse sides: in the southern portions of Death Valley is a well paved road leading past *Badwater* — at 282 feet below sea level, this is the lowest point in the northern hemisphere. Not far from here, an unpaved road leads to the *Devil's Golf Course,* an area with rugged cliff and salt formations.

The 9 mile long, one way *Artist Drive* leads through the foothills of the Black Mountains, the slopes of which are composed of coloured rock layers.

A similar landscape of rock formations begins at the southern end of Furnace Creek. The road leading to *Dante's View* is 24 miles long and has a number of points of interest along the way, for example, Zabriskie Point or Twenty Mule Team Canyon. At Dante's View, the elevation of 5,458 feet allows for a fascinating overall view of Death Valley, from the lowest point to the Sierra Nevada mountain range which borders the valley.

The oasis of *Furnace Creek* is the area most frequently visited and the hub of the National Monument. In addition to the Visitors Center, the Borax Museum is also located here, offering information on the mining and processing of this ore. The Visitor Center is open from the beginning of November to Easter from 8 am to 8 pm, and from 8 am to 5 pm during the rest of the year. At the extreme northern end of the desert, only 8 miles from Scotty's Castle, is the *Ubehebe Crater* with a diameter of 2,361 fee and a depth of 497 feet. This crater originates from a volcanic eruption which took place about 1,000 years ago. *Scotty's Castle* in Grapevine Canyon was built as the holiday residence of the wealthy industrialist Albert M. Johnson from Chicago in the 1920's. In 1970, the US government bought the estate and incorporated it into the national monument. Scotty's Castle is open from 9 am to 5 pm and offers tours. Admission costs $4 for adults and $2 for children between 6 and 11.

Death Valley National Monument / Practical Information

Accommodation

Camping: In the park, there are a total of nine campsites, although only three of theses are open all year: Furnace Creek, Mesquite Spring and Wildrose. The campsites Texas Spring, Sunset, and Stovepipe Wells are open from October to April; the campsites Emigrant, Thorndike and Mahogany, from May to September.

Prices range from $2 to $5.

Information: Tel: (619) 786-2332.

Hotels/Motels: Furnace Creek Inn, open October 14 to May 9, one and two persons $150 to $225, Tel: (619) 786-2345.

Furnace Creek Ranch, one and two persons from $60 to $90, an additional person costs $14, Tel: (619) 786-2345.

Stovepipe Wells Village, one and two persons from $50 to $60, an additional person costs $8.

Medical Care: Within the desert park, the park rangers will be of assistance. Outside the park, there is a first aid station in Beatty on the US 95, in Trona on State Route 178 and in Shoshone on State Road 127. Hospitals can be found in Lone Pine on US 395 (38 miles), in Las Vegas (142 miles) and in Tonopah on US 95 (91 miles).

Restaurants: Restaurant, coffee shop and cafeteria at the Furnace Creek Ranch; prices from $6 to $16. The restaurant is closed from June to August. The restaurant in Stovepipe Wells Village has prices from $8 to $15.

Shopping: Groceries can be found in stores in Furnace Creek, Stovepipe Wells Village and at the service stations in Furnace Creek, Stovepipe Wells Village and Scotty's Castle.

Sports

Cycling: Bicycles can be rented in Furnace Creek.

Golf: There is an 18-hole golf course in the oasis of Furnace Creek.

Tennis: The Furnace Creek Hotel has four tennis courts and the Furnace Creek Ranch has 2 tennis courts.

Travelling There: When coming from Las Vegas, one can take US 95 to the east entrance to the park. The State Roads 373 and 190 via Death Valley Junction, the 374 via Daylight Pass and 267 in the north (to Scotty's Castle) lead into the valley.

Las Vegas — Furnace Creek 141 miles.
From the west side via Lone Pine or Olancha (US 395) State Road 136 or 139 or via China Lake, State Road 178 lead into the park. The distance from all of the above mentioned towns to Furnace Creek is about 90 miles. The State Road 127 leads off from Interstate 15 near baker to Shoshone. From there, the 178 leads over Jubilee Pass to the southeast entrance not far from Ashford Mill.

Shoshone — Furnace Creek 70 miles;

Los Angeles — Furnace Creek 318 miles;

San Francisco — Furnace Creek 528 miles.

Important Addresses: Death Valley National Monument, Death Valley, CA 92328. Visitor Center in Furnace Creek, Tel: (619) 786-2331.

Death Valley is known as "the most beautiful desert in the world"

Discounts

Students with an international or US student identification card can get discounts of up to 30% in most museums, theatres and larger aquariums, etc. Children under six will also receive discounts on admission. Sometimes discounts are made dependent on height — an original alternative. Senior citizens, especially retirees, receive discounts similar to the students and a "Golden Age Passport" free of charge, which entitles the holder to free admission to all national parks as well as discounted fees at the campsites within the parks.

Driving Licence →*Travel in California*

A must for every visitor to California — the spectacular rock formations at Zabiskie Point in Death Valley

Economy

Around half of the entire state economy comes from the factories, especially important for transport. Occupying the dominant position, especially in Los Angeles and San Diego, is the aerospace industry. Following second on the scale is the agricultural sector, California being the leading state for agricultural production in the United States. The San Joaquin Valley has especially high yields. In third place is the tourism industry. Following this are the expanding computer industry concentrated in Silicon Valley and Palo Alto, the wood industry, and the entertainment and media industries, focussed around Hollywood.

Electricity

Those travelling to the United States from foreign countries should note that the electrical voltage is 110-120 volts. For this reason, it might be necessary to bring along the appropriate electrical adapters. Most laptop computers have an electrical converter chip and/or battery buffer making it necessary to only have the appropriate plug adapter.

Embassies →*Consulates*

Entertainment

In California, there truly is no business like show business. What can be especially emphasised are the large amusement parks like Disneyland and the film studios in Hollywood (→*Los Angeles),* but even simply visiting one of the large cinema palaces in Hollywood can be quite an experience. In San Francisco, there are pubs and bars to suit every taste. Often, live music is performed in many cafés, pubs and bars. There is also no shortage of discotheques in the large cities. On the more cultural side, the larger cities offer theatre, ballet and opera, although this is more so the case in San Francisco than in Los Angeles. In Los Angles, the film industry dominates the entertainment scene.

Information on entertainment and special events is available in the tourist information offices (→*Tourist Information and individual entries),* in the entertainment section of daily newspapers or in the programme brochures, usually available free of charge.

Geography

The fundamental and developmental situation of this geologically striking state seems heavily dependent on destiny. The earth's crust is assumed to be comprised of twelve gigantic plates, the so-called tectonic plates. These "float" on the cushion of magma in the inner recesses of the earth, sometimes moving against one another. Two of these plates come together at the 750 mile long San Andreas fault, a site at which around 11,000 seismic disturbances are registered per year. Luckily, the greatest portion of these are indiscernible without sensitive equipment. The Pacific Plate with the ocean and the southern coastal region around Los Angeles drifts about an inch or two to the north each year, while the North American Plate with eastern California and San Francisco moves southward at the same rate. At some points, the plates cannot move against each other and tension builds. When they then do break loose, they do so in a way similar to a catapult. In such instances, the unimaginable energy of an earthquake is set loose, causing disastrous natural catastrophes like in 1857 at Tejon Pass, or on April 18, 1906 or October 17, 1989 in San Francisco. The seismologists, in the end, always find themselves confronted by the same dilemma. They know where the dangerous zones are, they understand the interdependent causes and can even predict the approximate intensity of an expected earthquake. It is only the exact time that cannot be foretold. This can only be estimated using theoretical principals of probability.

Despite this, the residents of California, the most densely populated state in the US, remain astonishingly calm and composed. Even more people move to California each year — California is, after all, a beautiful, diverse and fascinating state.

The Pacific coast in the northern portions of the state is rugged, sometimes steep, falling off sharply to the ocean below, while in the south, the coast slopes off gently to the ocean in the form of beautiful beaches. The entire coastline has three large bays, which serve as natural harbours: Humboldt Bay, San Francisco Bay and San Diego Bay. Mountain ranges run parallel to the coastline, which have a large influence on the climate of California (→Climate). The Coast Ranges follow directly near the coastline from the northwest southwards to Los Angeles. Further inland, the Sierra

Nevadas start in the northeastern regions of California and go down almost to Bakersfield. This impressive mountain range is predominantly composed of granite, increasing in altitude gradually from the west to its magnificent summits and then usually falling off sharply to the east.

The Sierra Nevada mountain range is especially impressive between Sequoia National Park and the beautiful alpine lake of Lake Tahoe. It is not by chance that beautiful national parks are located in this area *(→Yosemite National Park, Kings Canyon, Sequoia National Park)* as well as other majestic nature areas.

In the northeastern regions of California, the Sierra Nevadas include a number of volcanoes. None of these are still active, though. The two largest and most widely known are Mount Lassen *(→Lassen Volcanic National Park)* and the yet loftier Mount Shasta.

Between these two mountain ranges, the coastal ranges and the Sierra

Lush vegetation is characteristic for many regions of California

Nevadas, is a valley which extends approximately 410 miles with a width ranging between 40 and 50 miles. This Central Valley is subdivided into the northern Sacramento Valley and the southern San Joaquin Valley. The Sacramento and San Joaquin rivers provide water for this extensive and fertile valley before they both empty into the San Francisco Bay. The southeastern regions of California are predominantly characterised by deserts. Among these are →*Death Valley National Monument* on the California border to Nevada, the Mojave Desert, and finally to the south of these, the fascinating →*Joshua Tree National Monument* as well as the →*Anza Borrego Desert State Park.*

Health Insurance

Payment for medical and dental treatment is expected in advance, although insufficient funds is not a reason for refusing treatment in emergencies. A credit card can definitely be helpful with large sums for treatment. It is also recommended to take out a supplemental travel health insurance policy for the duration of one's trip. Most major insurance companies and some airlines and credit card companies offer such policies. Travel insurance is usually quite reasonably priced and is limited to the exact dates of travel.

History

The first European to land on the Californian coast was the Portuguese navigator Ivan Rodriguez Cabrillo. He had embarked under the auspices of the Spanish crown to land on the coast near what is now San Diego. Today, the Castillo National Monument stands at this site as a reminder of this historical event.

The famous English explorer Sir Francis Drake was to follow later in 1579, landing near →*Point Reyes* and declaring the land "New Albion" for his queen, Elizabeth I. The present name of the state first came into being with the arrival of Sebastian Vizcaino, who explored the coastline extensively, also giving Monterey and San Diego their names. Although this all took place under the flag and authority of the Spanish crown, the European power paid little attention to this remote province for the subsequent

60 years. This was to change dramatically when the Spanish King Carlos felt threatened by the ever increasing attacks by England and Russia. In 1768, the Spaniard Gaspar de Portola lead an expedition which would lay claim to the entire coastline, including the San Francisco Bay area. In accordance with Spanish tradition, his expedition also included representatives of the church, under the leadership of the two Franciscans Juniper Serra and Fermin Lasuen, who founded a number of missions in the name of the Catholic Church. The two Padres account for the establishment of nine missions each. In 1823, 21 Christian missions had already been established between San Diego and Sonoma, north of San Pablo Bay. In addition to these missions, military bases called "Presidios" in San Diego, Santa Barbara and San Francisco exerted power and influence over the various Indian tribes in California.

In 1777, the first civilian settlement was founded in San Jose. The founding of Los Angeles would follow one year later. The attempt made by the Russians to participate in developing California by establishing Fort Ross, 60 miles north of San Francisco was destined to fail. In 1841, this stronghold had to be abandoned. Today, this fortress is the focal point of a state historic park.

The province of California became a part of Mexico resulting from the war of independence in 1822. But as early as 1840, there were already militant attempts by the United States to take control of this region. The Bear Flag Revolt of 1846 was the military peak of these efforts. It was, however, only after the end of the Mexican American War that California became a territory of the United States with the Treaty of Guadalupe Hidalgo on February, 1848. In 1850, California became the 31st state in the union. This development must be considered in light of that which made California so famous: the first gold was discovered in California in 1842 north of Los Angeles. This, followed by additional discoveries in the American River near Colma at the end of January 1848 prompted an unprecedented exodus. From this point on, the rumour and enticement of gold was to change the land as well as the people. It is not widely known that gold continued to be mined in California up until the middle of the twentieth century from productive mines. Meanwhile, the role of former importance of gold has been replaced with oil and natural gas.

Two factors influenced the development of California, especially during the first half of the 20th century, and continue to influence its character even today. These were the mass exodus to California and the invention of the automobile. Facets of California can be explained by these factors like the rich ethnic and cultural diversity, the openness and tolerance, the creative energy and strength and the unsurpassed mobility of Californians. For those who flock to California even today, the reputation and mystique of this state, namely one that holds the promise of a better and more pleasant life, plays an important role.

Holidays and Celebrations

The national holidays are usually observed on a Monday, making it possible for many to take a short trip during the long weekend. Visitors should avoid the main highways, national parks and recreation areas on these days because they will always be extremely congested.

National Holidays
January 1: New Year's Day;
Third Monday in January: Martin Luther King Jr.'s Birthday;
Third Monday in February: President's Day (celebrating George Washington's and Abraham Lincoln's Birthdays);
Easter Sunday;
Last Monday in May: Memorial Day;
July 4: Independence Day;
First Monday in September: Labor Day;
Second Monday in October: Columbus Day;
Fourth Monday in October: Veterans' Day;
Fourth Thursday in November: Thanksgiving Day;
December 25: Christmas Day.

On official holidays, with the exception of Easter, Christmas and New Year's Day, many stores remain open.

In addition, there are a number of unofficial holidays like Cinco de Mayo (May 5), Mexico's independence from Spain, celebrated in many areas in and around Los Angeles.

Holiday Apartments →*Accommodation*

Hospitals

In California, there is a hospital in almost every city, providing high standards in medical care. In addition, almost every national park has first aid stations. Many of the larger cities will have medical and dental referral services, which will be able to recommend physicians and dentists.
→*Medical Care, Health Insurance*

Insurance

There are travel insurance policies available, covering just about everything. Minimum travel coverage should include travel health, accident and baggage insurance. These can often be combined into a relatively inexpensive insurance package which is limited to the exact dates of travel. If one should require treatment in a hospital or clinic, payment is expected in cash or by credit card. In-patient treatment costs range from $400 to $600 per day, which makes not only a credit card handy in this situation, but an insurance policy which covers these costs as well.

This is also true in the case of travel liability insurance. The liability insurance included in most travel packages does not cover liability to the owner, holder or driver of a motorised vehicle, aircraft or motorised boat, due to damages resulting from the use of the vehicle. This makes it wise to opt for the additional insurance coverage available when renting a vehicle. Depending on the company, this ranges from $8 to $18 per day. Without this, coverage is usually limited to only $25,000.

Further information is available through insurance companies, automobile clubs or the American Underwriters and the AAA, which are represented in most larger cities in the United States.

American International Underwriters, 70 Pine Street, New York, New York 10005.

American Automobile Association, Travel Insurance Department, 8111 Gatehouse Road, Falls Church, Virginia 22047.

Joshua Tree National Monument

The desert area of Joshua Tree National Monument has a lot to offer for nature lovers. Not only are there numerous and vastly different types of cactus plants, giving the landscape its character, but also rugged mountains and barren granite monoliths, composing a fascinating overall picture. This landscape marks the meeting point of two different deserts and thus, two different ecosystems, set apart from each other mainly by their differing elevations. Only few areas in the world make the contrast in altitude so apparent as here. The Colorado Desert lies below 3,000 feet above sea level and extends over the eastern half of the park. This is where fascinating desert vegetation grows. In the western half of the national monument, located at a higher altitude, is the cooler Mojave Desert. Here, one will find the bizarre Joshua trees, which give the national monument its name. The trees themselves were given their name by the Mormons in the 19th century when journeying to the area east of present-day Palm Springs. These strange plants reminded them of Joshua, leading the chosen people to the promised land with outstretched arms. Entire forests of these trees often extend over miles in this region. One should, however, be cautious when roaming through this area because, in addition to the Joshua trees, there are also cholla cactus plants, also called the jumping teddy bear. These do in fact look like teddy bears, albeit less cuddly. One should keep a distance from these plants because ground vibrations cause them to release thorny balls, which attach themselves to the skin. Joshua Tree National Monument is 140 miles east of Los Angeles and is best reached via Interstate 10 to Cottonwood Spring. From the north, there is also an entrance from US 62 at Twentynine Palms. The entrances to the national monument are open daily from 8 am to 5 pm. The entrance at Twentynine Palms also has a visitor centre with information on flora, fauna and the geographical history of the park. Admission to the park costs $5 per vehicle.

Information: Superintendent Joshua Tree National Monument, 74485 National Monument Drive, Twentynine Palms, California 92277, Tel: (619) 367-7511.

Julian

A trip to Julian, located approximately 60 miles northeast of San Diego and bordering on the →*Anza Borrego Desert State Park,* leads into a pretty little town of approximately 1,300, which traces its origins back to the gold rush. It experienced the peak of the gold rush era during the 1870's. Today, there is still a lot which points to this period. This is especially true of the Eagle and Highpeak gold mines (tours are offered) and the Pioneer Museum (open only during weekends and holidays from 10 am to 4 pm). Tours through the gold mines cost $6 for adults and $3 for those under 16 years of age. Information is available by contacting Tel: (619) 765-9921.

Accommodation

Julian Lodge, 2720 C Street, $100 to $120, Tel: (619) 765-1420.

Lake Tahoe

The deep blue, alpine Lake Tahoe lies at an altitude of 6,230 feet and covers area of 202 square miles. It is 22 miles long and 12 miles wide with an astonishing depth of almost 1.000 feet. However, it is not these statistics which make this lake so attractive to tourists. It is more so the unusual contrast between the relaxing and beautiful landscape and the hectic bustle of the gambling towns located on the eastern shores of the lake. About a third of the lake's area lies in the state of Nevada, which is especially apparent in the small city of Stateline on the southeastern shores of the lake. Only a stone-throw away, the city of South Lake Tahoe in California is the largest city on the southern shores and is simultaneously the most popular destination for tourists.

A drive around the lake on the 72 mile long shoreline road is one of the most popular sightseeing trips in this area. Along the way, one will drive through a number of small, interesting towns and will come across several attractions like Vikingsholm, a replica of a Viking fortress from the 19th century, located in Emerald Bay State Park. It is open from the beginning of July to the beginning of September daily from 10 am to 4 pm, admission is $1.

Another tourist attraction is the famous Ponderosa Ranch and the adjacent Western Theme Park. This set for the Bonanza television series can be toured, including demonstrations of the stunts and equipment used in the production of the television series. Tours are offered in summer from 10 am to 7 pm, prices for adults is $5, children from 5 to 11 years of age $4. Information: Tel: (702) 831-0691.

The shoreline road on the eastern side of the lake in Nevada, leads almost up to Zephyr Cove. The Carson mountain range almost reaches to the water at this point. From this location, one will have a magnificent view of the lake, with the opportunity of taking photographs or finding a secluded bay for swimming.

The Lake Tahoe area is considered one of the most beautiful winter sports areas in the United States. The most renowned ski areas are Squaw Valley, which hosted the winter Olympic games in 1960, and Heavenly Valley, accessible via South Lake Tahoe. The gondola is in operation during the summer. The breathtaking view from the summit restaurant makes a ride on the gondola well worthwhile.

Lake Tahoe / Practical Information

Accommodation

Camping: There are a number of campsites all along the lakeshore. Most can be found in and around the city of South Lake Tahoe. Prices range from $14 to $20.

Eldorado Campground, 170 tent and RV sites, South Lake Tahoe on US 50, Tel: (916) 544-3317 and (916) 537-2059.

KOA Campground, 68 tent and RV sites, in Meyers on US 50, Tel: (916) 577-3693.

Tahoe Paradise Campground, 75 tent and RV sites, on Upper Truckee River on US 50, Tel: (916) 541-9983.

Tahoe Pines Campground, 75 tent and RV sites, 11 miles from the state line on US 50, Tel: (916) 577-1635.

Tahoe Valley Recreation Campground, 288 tent and RV sites, "Y" of "C" Street, Tel: (916) 541-2222.

Hikers receive a discount at these campsites.

Hotels/Motels: These are available in such large numbers that one will have no problems in finding lodging even without reservations. Most of these can be found in south Lake Tahoe along US 50. Prices start at $30 for two persons, a third person will pay around $6.

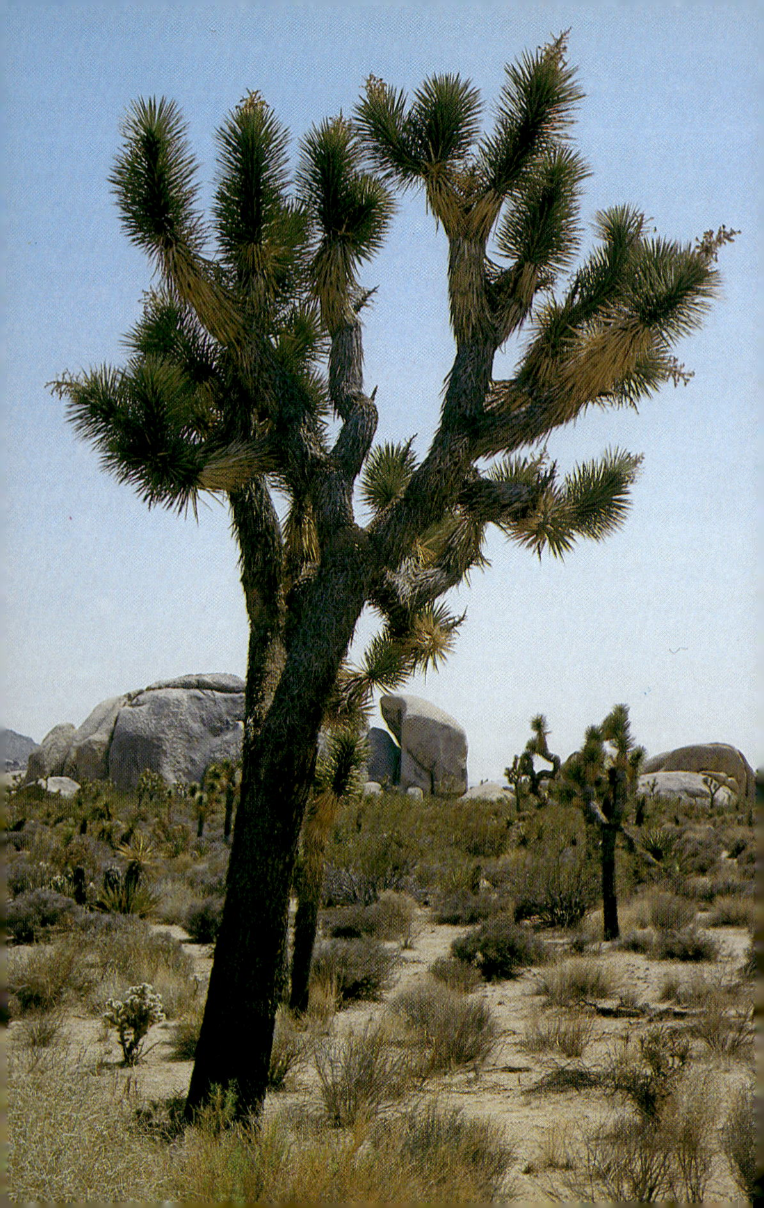

Lake Tahoe

Youth Hostel: South Lake Tahoe Hostel, $9 for members, 1043 Martin Street, Tel: (916) 544-3834.

Excursions

Bus: The three bus lines Grayline Tours, Travel Systems and Safaris & Tours offer excursions into the surrounding regions. Popular destinations are Reno, Virginia City and Carson City, all located in Nevada.

Grayline Tours, P.O. Box 3853, Stateline, Nevada 89449, Tel: (702) 588-6688.

Safaris & Tours, P.O. Box 5469, Incline Village, Nevada 89450, Tel: (702) 831-4567.

Travel Systems, P.O. Box 1667, Zephyr Cove, Nevada 89448, Tel: (702) 588-5656.

Boat: Boat tours start at Zephyr Cove, Tahoe City and South Lake Tahoe, usually limited to the months from May to September. These tours last between 2 and 4 hours and cost between $9 and $25. Further information is available and reservations can be made by calling:

Zephyr Cove, Nevada, (702) 588-3508,

Tahoe City, California, Tel: (916) 541-0141,

South Lake Tahoe, California, Tel: (916) 541-4652 and (916) 541-3364,

Lake Tahoe Cruises, P.O. Box 14327, South Lake Tahoe, CA 95702.

Restaurants: The selection of good as well as inexpensive restaurants is very large. This is especially true in the casino towns. Very popular are also the breakfast, lunch and dinner buffets which are usually offered in most of the casinos as a special service to their clientele.

Shopping: Supermarkets with a large selection can be found especially in the larger towns like South Lake Tahoe and Incline Village.

Sports

Horseback Riding: Horseback tours are offered at the Bonanza Farm and the Camp Richardson Corral. Prices range from $15 to $18 per hour.

Swimming: There are numerous swimming beaches all along the shores of the lake. However, most do charge admission. The bays along the eastern shore are very nice and free of charge. The water temperature is usually a pleasant 68 °F.

◀ *The Joshua Tree National Monument was named after this impressive and bizarrely shaped tree*

Tennis: The following tennis courts are free of charge: Incline High School, Kings Beach Elementary School on Steelhead Street in Kings Beach, North Tahoe High School on Polaris Street east of Tahoe City, Tahoe Lake School on Grove Street in Tahoe City, Zephyr Cove Park on Warrior Way, Kilner Park south of Sunnyside, Sugar Pine Point State Park between Meek's Bay and Homewood on State Road 89.

Travelling There: This mountain lake lies in the middle of the Sierra Nevada Mountains, 206 miles east of San Francisco and 35 miles southwest of the gambling city of Reno Nevada. From Interstate 80, State Roads 89 and 267 lead up to the Lake. From the south, on can reach the southern Lake Tahoe region via US 50.

Important Addresses

Information: Lake Tahoe basin Management Unit, P.O. Box 8465, South Lake Tahoe, CA 95731, Tel: (916) 544-6420.

A visitor centre can be found around 3 miles northwest of South Lake Tahoe between Camp Richardson and Emerald Bay on State Road 89. It is open daily from 8 am to 6 pm during the summer, Tel: (916) 541-0209.

Lassen Volcanic National Park

The Lassen Volcanic National Park is located in a region in which volcanic activity can be traced back 25 million years.

In the period from 1914 to 1921, this area was, geologically speaking, very active with a total of 289 eruptions, which destroyed all vegetation within a radius of twenty miles. Bubbling mud pots, hot springs and obvious remnants of the past eruptions led to the establishment of this national park in 1916, after which, interest in this portion of the southern Cascade mountain range in the northern regions of California grew rapidly.

Lassen Volcanic National Park / Sights

Most of the points of interest are concentrated along the eighty mile long park road at the base of Lassen Peak with an altitude of 10,422 feet above sea level. What is especially impressive is the southern portion of the park. Here, the *Sulphur Works Thermal Area* and the one mile long *Bumpass Hell Pass* gives a good impression of the churning disquiet of this inactive volcano. Also very lovely is the 2½ mile *Lassen Peak Mountain Pass,* which leads a mile beyond Lake Helen to the edge of the volcano. The *Devastated Area* above the halfway point along the park road illustrates quite clearly the destructive energy set loose by the eruption of Lassen Peak in May of 1914. At the northern of this region is the massive black boulder of lava, weighing approximately 120 metric tons, which the eruption catapulted almost four miles to this location.

Admission to the national park costs $5 per vehicle.

Lassen Volcanic National Park / Practical Information
Accommodation
Activities: Within the park, there is an extensive network of hiking trails. These trails are the best way of exploring the park. One can get specific information on individual trails and activities in the park headquarters. This is located about one mile west of Mineral on State Road 36. The ranger programme includes everything from educational hikes and lectures to campfire talks at the camping sites. Winter sports facilities are located near the northwest entrance.

Camping: Within the park, there are three camping sites which can be recommended: Butte Lake Campground, the Manzanita Lake Campground and the North Summit Lake Campground. All three cost $5 to $7. Depending on the weather conditions, these camping sites are open from June to October. Information: (916) 335-4266 and (916) 595-4444 (North Summit).

Motels: Drakesbad Guest Ranch, at the end of Warner Valley Road, one and two persons $70 to $120, $40 for an additional person, small cottages are available for up to four persons for $55 to $155.

Medical Care: Within the national park, the visitor centers and the ranger stations are equipped to provide first aid. The nearest hospitals outside the park are in Chester on State Route 36 (about 36 miles from the southern entrance to the park) and in Burney on State Route 44 (about 45 miles from the northern entrance to the park).

Ranger Stations: At Sulphur Works (southern entrance), Summit Lake, Juniper Lake, Horseshoe Lake, Drakesbad and near the Manzanita Lake at the north entrance.

Travelling There: By car, visitors can reach the northwest entrance to the park on State Road 44 after about 50 miles; from Red Bluff, it is about 50 miles to the southwest park entrance after driving about 47 miles. Both entrances are on Interstate 5.

The nearest airports are located in Redding and Chico. Buses operate on weekdays from Red Bluff or Susanville to Mineral, a small town near the southwestern entrance to the park.

Important Addresses: Superintendent, Lassen Volcanic National Park, P.O. Box 100, Mineral, CA 96063, Tel: (916) 595-4444.

Two visitor centers are located at each of the entrances to the park in the north and southwest.

Literature

Non-Fiction
Eagle, Dolan H. Jr., *The Earth is Our Mother,* Trees Company Press.
- The history of the Native Americans in California from their beginnings to the present, including a comprehensive list of Native American holidays and festivals (with date and location) and existing reservations.

California Gold: Story of the Rush to Riches, Zanel Publications.
- Documenting the wild era of the gold rush with numerous and interesting original documents.

California Ghost Town Trails, Gem Guide Books.
- Lists all of the ghost towns with individual and descriptive background information as well as a description of what awaits the visitor today.

Fiction
Mark Twain, *The Celebrated Jumping Frog of Calavaras County and Other Stories,* 1865.

Mark Twain, *Roughing It,* 1872.

Jack London, *Martin Eden,* 1909.

Jack London, *John Barleycorn,* 1913.

Nathaniel West, *The Day of the Locust,* 1939.

John Steinbeck, *The Grapes of Wrath,* 1939.

F. Scott Fitzgerald, *The Last Tycoon,* 1940.

John Steinbeck, *Cannery Row,* 1944 *(→Monterey).*

Los Angeles

In 1847, Filipe de Neve, along with a group of eleven families, founded a settlement where now the Olvera Street and Historic Park are located. This settlement was named "El Pueblo des Nuestra Señora la Reina de Los Angeles de Porciuncula," in English, "the city of our lady, the queen among the angels." This long chain of words was quickly shortened to Los Angeles, and then to LA. This city is one which does not have the best reputation with many Americans and whose popularity remains limited. It has taken on the dimensions of a megalopolis with an area of 472 square miles and is home to over eight million people, when the suburbs are included. Almost 100 languages are spoken by the residents.

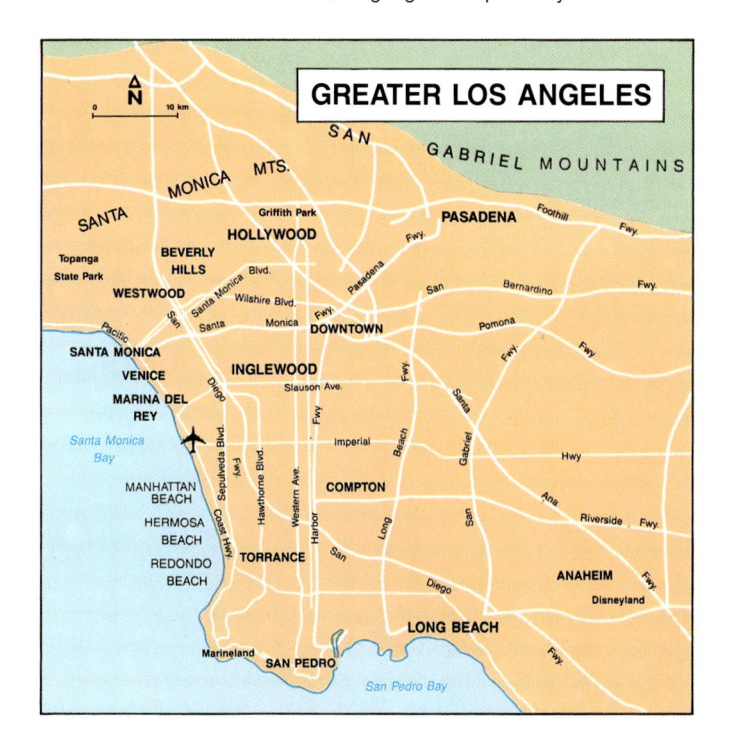

Such a mix of people and cultures cannot be found anywhere else in the United States. One of the leading factors in this development is the existence of the oil, textile, automobile and electronic industries in this state as well as the lure and glamour of Hollywood.

California's reputation and the hope of employment with better pay has always acted as a powerful magnet for domestic and foreign workers — more, in fact than the economy can handle. If one includes the influence of the two universities, the 100 year old University of Southern California (USC) and the University of California at Los Angeles (UCLA), founded in 1919, then the city is constituted as follows: there is a crass difference in social standing between the wealthy and the poor with tension growing as obvious poverty is on the rise. In addition to this, Los Angeles has difficulty in projecting its own identity or to identify with a specific character. On the other hand, this diversity expands on the already numerous attractions offered visitors with even more attractions. There is so much to see in Los Angeles that one will have to make a strict choice of which to visit and stick to those choices. It is for good reason and not only due to Hollywood that Los Angeles is called the "entertainment capital" of the United States.

Los Angeles / Sights

Chinatown: Chinatown centers around the Mandarin Plaza Mall, 970 North Broadway. It is not quite as lively or at interesting as Chinatown in New York or San Francisco, but it is still worth visiting.

Disneyland: This amusement park par excellence is a must for anyone visiting Los Angeles. It is comprised of six theme parks, each with a number of ingenious attractions. One should definitely plan to spend an entire day in Disneyland and to arrive as early as possible. It is best to arrive at the park's main entrance at 9 am when it opens and begin with the most popular attractions. These include: the jungle cruise, the haunted mansion, Big Thunder Mountain Railroad, the Matterhorn Bobsleds, Space Mountain, Splash Mountain and Star Tours. One should avoid the park during weekends because then it is often hopelessly overcrowded. Disneyland is located in Anaheim, directly on the Santa Ana Freeway (I-5) at 1313 Harbor Boulevard, about 34 miles south of the downtown Los

Los Angeles

Angeles area. Admission: 3-day pass $72.50 for adults, children 5 to 11 $50.50; 2-day pass $50 for adults, $40 for children; one-day pass $27.50 for adults and $22.50 for children. Disneyland is open from the middle of June to the middle of September, Sunday to Friday from 9 am until midnight, Saturdays from 9 am to 1 am. From the middle of September to the middle of June, it is open Wednesday to Friday from 10 am to 6 pm and Saturdays and Sundays from 9 am to 7 pm. These times are subject to slight changes.

Information is available by contacting: Disneyland Guest Relations, P.O. Box 3232, Anaheim, California 92803, Tel: (714) 999-4565.

Downtown Los Angeles: The center of town with its skyscrapers seems to be intent on polishing up its smudged image with power and high finance. This seems to be the motivation the expansion of the Convention Center to include the 73-story First Interstate World Center, which, upon completion, will be the tallest building on the west coast.

In addition, the following buildings are worth seeing in the downtown area:

City Hall, 200 North Spring and First Street. From the observation platform of this 450 foot tall building, one has a nice view of the downtown area.

Music Center, First Street and Grand Avenue. This is the home of the Los Angeles Philharmonic Orchestra, the Joffrey Ballet Los Angeles/New York, the Los Angeles Master Chorale and the Light Opera, which becomes the focus of attention when the Academy of Motion Picture Arts & Sciences awards its Oscars in the famous Dorothy Chandler Pavillion. Tours lasting about an hour are offered free of charge. One must, however, make reservations in advance during the tourist season, Tel: (213) 972-7483; Information about special events and performances, Tel: (213) 972-7211.

Watts Towers, 1765 East 107th Street in Watts, south of the downtown area. Measuring between 50 and 100 feet, these "towers" were created by the Italian immigrant Simon Rodia. It took him 33 years to complete his work of art comprised of broken tiles, broken bottles, parts of old bed frames, seashells, iron, cement and other refuse. Tel: (213) 569-8181.

Westin Bonaventure, 404 South Figueroa Street. This hotel and shopping complex with a bar and revolving restaurant on its top floor is very much worth seeing. It has glass elevators both on the inside and outside of the building, and gained fame through the Mel Brooks film "High Anxiety." The hotel's prices start at $150 per night. Tel: (213) 624-1000.

El Pueblo de Los Angeles State Historic Park: In this, the birthplace of Los Angeles, a number of historical buildings have been restored. The oldest is the *Avila Adobe,* from the year 1818. The *Olvera Street,* is also located in this district and makes up the center of the colourful Mexican area. From the Visitor Center *(→Important Addresses, this entry),* there are tours offered, weekdays from 10 am to 3 pm and during weekends from 10 am to 4:30 pm, Tel: (213) 628-1274.

Hollywood: The glamour of Hollywood consists of a great deal of nostalgia. How else can one describe the "Walk of Fame," the sidewalk on Hollywood Boulevard with over 1800 brass stars with the names of famous film greats. In the cement in front of Mann's Chinese Theater (formerly Grauman's) are the hand and footprints as well as the autographs of the stars of the silver screen. This idea is said to have come from the actress Norma Talmadge, who accidentally stepped in the wet cement before climbing

Main Street, USA in Disneyland leads to the attractions of this world famous theme park

into her car parked in front of this interesting building. Outshining everything else are the huge letters on the mountainside spelling out Hollywood. A good place to take a photograph of this is from Deronda Drive.

A tour of the *Universal Studios* will reveal some of the tricks of the film trade. The stunt, animal and other shows are highly entertaining.

Admission: Adults $24, children from 3 to 11 $18.50. The extensive grounds are found near the Hollywood Freeway at 3900 Lankershim Boulevard in Universal City, Tel: (818) 508-9600.

A visit to a *television show* is one of the most interesting things that Los Angeles has to offer. Admission tickets can be had without any problems, but one should definitely call beforehand for information:

ABC-TV, 4151 Prospect Avenue, Hollywood, California 90027, Tel: (213) 557-4396. Tickets are available here Monday to Friday from 9 am to 5 pm

Audiences Unlimited, 5746 Sunset Boulevard, Tel: (818) 506-0043. Tickets are available Monday to Friday from 8 am to 4 pm.

Audiences Associates, 1680 Vine Street, Hollywood, California 90028, Tel: (213) 467-4697.

CBS-TV, 7800 Beverly Boulevard, Los Angeles, California 90036, Tel: (213) 852-4002. Tickets are available Monday to Friday from 9 am to 5 pm, Saturdays and Sundays from 10 am to 5 pm.

NBC-TV, 3000 West Alameda Avenue, Burbank, California 91523, Tel: (818) 840-3537. Tickets are available Monday to Friday from 8:30 am to 5 pm, Saturdays and Sundays from 9:30 am to 4 pm.

Paramount Audience Shows, 780 North Gower Street, Los Angeles, California 90038, Tel: (213) 468-5575.

Hollywood Bowl, 2301 North Highland Avenue. In this famous and beautifully located amphitheatre seats an audience of almost 18,000. From July 1 to September 15, the Los Angeles Philharmonic Orchestra holds concerts here. Concerts are on Tuesdays, Thursdays, Fridays and Saturdays at 8:30 pm, Tel: (213) 850-2000.

Beverly Hills: This elegant area of town is known for its pompous mansions some of which belong to film and television stars as well as its exclusive boutiques and restaurants on Rodeo Drive. General maps and maps of especially interesting or famous mansions are available at the

Beverly Hills Tourist Information Office at 239 South Beverly Drive, Tel: (213) 271-8174 or 1-800-345-2210.

Melrose Avenue: South of Hollywood, between Highland Avenue and Doheny Drive, the trend-setters, yuppies, punks and hippies frequent the boutiques, galleries, shops, theatres, restaurants and bars — to see people and be seen.

Knott's Berry Farm: This 153 acre amusement park is located about 8 miles northwest of Disneyland at 8039 Beach Boulevard. In this amusement park, there are, in addition to an *Old West Ghost Town,* a *Mexican Fiesta Village, Roaring 20's, Knott's Air Field* and *Snoopy Camp.* One very popular attraction is the parachute jump, a jump with a secured parachute from a height of twenty stories.

Knott's Berry Farm is open from the end of May to the beginning of September from 10 am to midnight, Admission $18.

Venice Beach: This former hippie and artists centre between Santa Monica and the Los Angeles International Airport is still a meeting place for colourful individualists, who sell handicrafts and various other articles in small shops, booths and stands. Others present their bodies for public evaluation at Muscle Beach and street musicians provide lively and colourful street theater free of charge.

Los Angeles / Practical Information

Accommodation

Camping: Malibu Beach RV Park, 40 tent and 125 RV sites, four persons from $25 to $30, additional person $3, 25801 Pacific Highway 1, Tel: (213) 456-6052. Leo Carillo State Beach, 138 tent and RV sites, $12 per site, 9000 Pacific Highway 1, Tel: (818) 706-1310. Los Angeles KOA Campground, 222 tent and RV sites priced from $22 to $30 for two persons, additional person $2 to $4 each, 15900 Olden Street in Sylmar, reservations are recommended, Tel: (818) 362-7785. Del Rio Mobile Home and RV Park, 60 RV sites, two persons $24 to $28, 5346 East Florence Avenue in Bell, Tel: (213) 560-2895. Shoreline RV Park, 70 RV sites, four persons from $24 to $30, additional person $3, 200 West Shoreline Drive in Long Beach, Tel: (213) 435-4960. Anaheim Junction Campground, 120 RV sites, two persons $24 to $30, additional person $3, 1230 South West Street,

Tel: (714) 533-0641. Anaheim KOA Campground, 221 RV sites, two persons $33, additional person $3 to $4, 1221 South West Street, Tel: (714) 533-7720. Anaheim Vacation Park, 222 RV sites, two persons from $24 to $30, additional person $3, 311 North Beach Boulevard in Anaheim, Tel: (714) 821-4311. Travellers World RV Park, 20 tent and 290 RV sites, two persons $20 to $26, additional person $3, 333 West Ball Road in Anaheim, Tel: (714) 991-0100.

Youth Hostels: Los Angeles International Hostel, $9 for members, 3601 South Gaffey Street, Building 613, in San Pedro, Tel: (213) 831-8109. Colonial Inn Hostel, $9 for members, 421 8th Street in Huntington Beach, Tel: (714) 536-3315. To get to this hostel from the Los Angeles International Airport, take bus number 232 to Long Beach and then bus number 1. Fullerton Hacienda Hostel, $9 for members, 1700 North Harbor Drive, Fullerton, Tel: (714) 738-3721. Interclub Hostel, from $12 in dormitories, 2221 Lincoln Boulevard in Venice Beach, Tel: (213) 305-0250. Santa Monica International Hostel, $9 for members, 1436 Second Street in Santa Monica, Tel: (213) 393-9913. Share-Tel International Hostel, $110 per week, 20 Brooks Avenue in Venice Beach, Tel: (213) 392-0325.

Hotels and Motels: Carmel House, one and two persons from $50, 201 Broadway in Santa Monica, Tel: (213) 451-2469. Crescent Hotel, one and two persons from $55, 403 North Crescent Drive in Beverly Hills, Tel: (213) 274-7595. Dutch Windmill Hospitality Home, one person from $28, 3505 Tuller Avenue in Santa Monica, Tel: (213) 390-5913. Royal Westwood Motel, one and two persons from $45, 2352 Westwood Boulevard near UCLA, Tel: (213) 475-4551. Seashore Motel, one and two persons from $45, 2637 Main Street in Santa Monica, Tel: (213) 392-2787.

Banks: Bank of America, Tel: (213) 389-3702.
California Federal Savings & Loan, Tel: (213) 932-4321, 1-800-421-0595.
Far East National Bank, Tel: (213) 253-0500.
First Interstate Bank, Tel: (213) 614-4111.
Pacific Stock Exchange, Tel: (213) 977-4500.
Security Pacific National Bank, Tel: (213) 345-6211.
Union Bank, Tel: (213) 236-5000.
Wells Fargo Bank, Tel: (213) 255-3300.

Beaches: The beach of this massive city is just as huge. Stretching over 44 miles, it connects the suburbs of Malibu, Santa Monica, Venice, Marina del Rey, Hermosa, Redondo and Palos Verdes. Malibu Beach in the northwest of the city is considered to be the most beautiful and most famous section in the Los Angeles area. From the downtown area, one can follow Sunset Boulevard down to Malibu.

Car Rental: The larger Car Rental Agencies have information desks at the airport in the baggage claim area. The exact addresses can be found in the yellow pages. In addition, there are also smaller, local agencies offering very reasonable prices.

Rent a Wreck, Tel: (213) 478-0678. Rent a Wreck, 11150 West Olympic Boulevard, Tel: (213) 479-3363. Rent a Wreck, 12868 Magnolia Boulevard, North Hollywood, Tel: (818) 762-3628. Bob Leach's Auto Rental, 4810 West Imperial Highway, Inglewood, Tel: (213) 673-2727.

Medical Care/Hospitals: Beverly Hills Medical Center, Tel: (213) 553-5155. Centinela Hospital Medical Center, 555 East Hardy Street, Inglewood, Tel: (213) 673-4660.

Channel Island Community Hospital, Oxnard, Tel: (805) 487-7941.

Memorial Hospital of Gordena, Tel: (213) 532-4200.

Mercy General Hospital, Santa Ana, Tel: (714) 754-5454.

Samaritan Health Center, 616 South Witmer Street, Los Angeles, Tel: (213) 977-2121.

Night Life/Entertainment: Night life in Los Angeles is concentrated in Hollywood along Sunset Strip, in Westwood and in Venice and Marina del Rey. In the Dorothy Chandler Pavillion are Los Angeles Philharmonic Orchestra concerts. In the Hollywood Bowl, the famous amphitheatre, "Symphonies under the Stars" are performed during the summer months. For current information on special events and performances, there is a 24 hour telephone recording: Tel: (213) 628-5857.

There is also information on special event in the entertainment sections of the *Sunday Los Angeles Times,* or the free brochures *Reader, L.A. Weekly, Key, Los Angeles,* and *Where,* which are available in most hotels.

Restaurants: One very popular alternative are the various restaurants and Cafés with tables outdoors or in the romantic courtyards of the Farmers

---

Comic book figures come to life in the Universal Film Studios in Los Angeles ▶

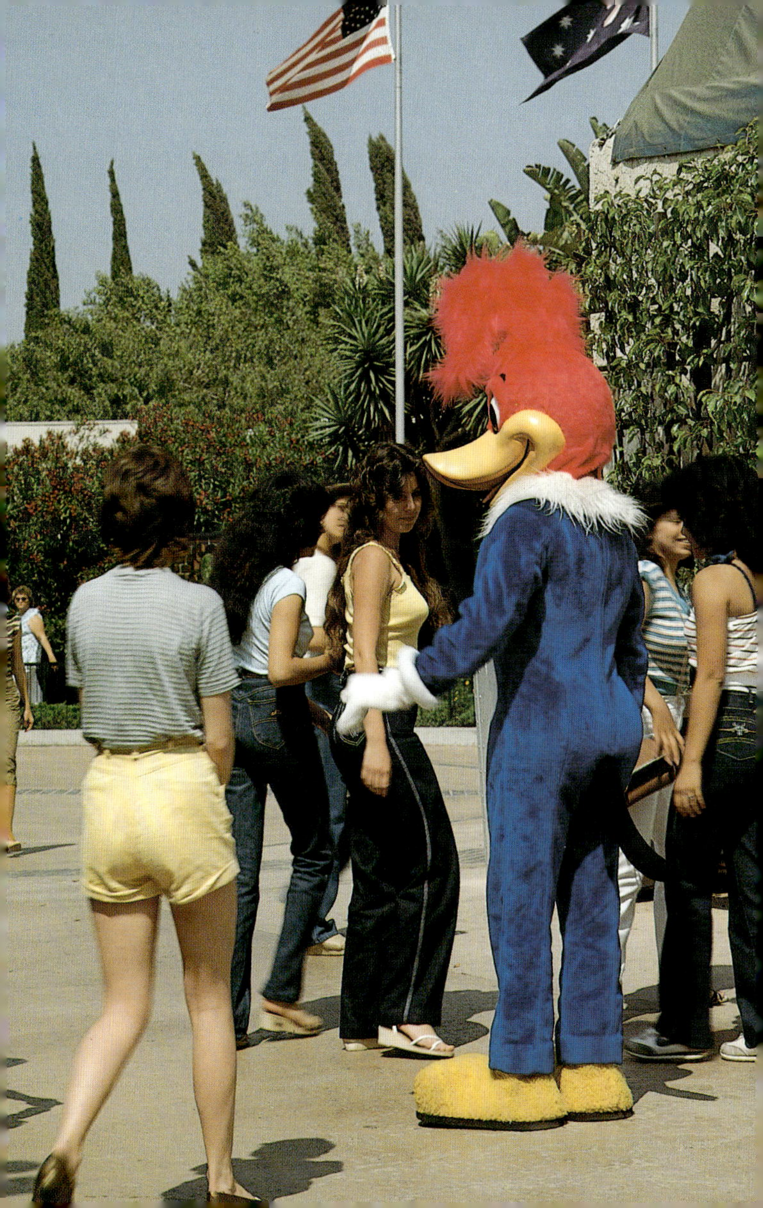

Market Zone, 6333 West Third Street and Fairfax Avenue, directly across from the CBS Studios, information: Tel: (213) 933-9211.

Restaurants in Anaheim: Benihana of Tokyo, 2100 East Ball Road, Anaheim California 92806, reservations are required, Tel: (714) 774-4940.

Restaurants in the Downtown Area: Ai Restaurant in the Rainbow Hotel, 536 South Hope Street, Los Angeles, California 90071, Tel: (213) 627-9941, inexpensive.

Alaska Hanten Chinese Restaurant, 123 South Weller Street, Los Angeles, California 90012, Tel: (213) 617-1100, middle price category.

Boy's Noodle Shop, 818 North Hill Street, Los Angeles, California 90012, Tel: (213) 617-7856, middle price category.

El Paseo de Los Angeles Restaurant, East 11 Olvera Street, Los Angeles, California 90012, Tel: (213) 626-1361, inexpensive.

Italian Kitchen, 420 West Eighth Street, Los Angeles, California 90014, Tel: (213) 622-9277, inexpensive.

Restaurants in Hollywood: Café Mondrian and Le Terrace, 8440 Sunset Boulevard, West Hollywood, California 90069, Tel: (213) 650-8999 or 1-800-321-4564, middle price category.

The Old Spaghetti Factory, 5939 Sunset Boulevard, Los Angeles, California 90028, Tel: (213) 469-7149, inexpensive.

Yamashiro Restaurant, 1999 North Sycamore Avenue, Hollywood, California, 90068, Tel: (213) 466-5125, middle price category.

Tick Tack Restaurant, 1716 North Cahaenga Boulevard, Tel: (213) 463-7576, inexpensive, offering complete meals.

Restaurants in Beverly Hills: Acapulco Mexican Restaurant, Westwood, 1109 Glendon Avenue, West Los Angeles, California 90024, Tel: (213) 208-3884, inexpensive.

Benihana of Tokyo, 38 North La Cienega Boulevard, Beverly Hills, California 90211, Tel: (213) 655-7311, middle price category.

Shopping: Souvenirs in all shapes and sizes can of course be found in the districts of Los Angeles most heavily frequented by tourists.

Farmers Market is a wonderfully lively open market where all types of foods and produce as well as articles of clothing and a variety of gifts can be purchased. The Farmers Market is located at 3rd Street and Fairfax Avenue, open Monday to Saturday from 9 am to 7 pm and Sundays from 10 am to 6 pm.

Good and inexpensive camping equipment can be purchased in the *Army and Navy Surplus Store,* 5649 Santa Monica Boulevard, Tel: (213) 469-0488.

The *Grand Central Market* is located on South Broadway which can compare with Farmers Market in atmosphere. It is open daily from 9 am to 6 pm and Saturdays from 10 am to 4 pm, offering an amazing variety of fruits and vegetables, meats and spices. In addition is the *Flower Mart,* Seventh and Wall Street, a huge wholesale flower warehouse.

Shopping Centers: Beverly Hills Center, 8500 Beverly Boulevard 500, Los Angeles, California 90048, Tel: (213) 845-0071. Bonaventura Shopping Gallery, 404 South Figueroa Street, Suite 370, Los Angeles, California 90071, Tel: (213) 687-0680. Dragon Gate Plaza, 818 North Hill Street, Los Angeles, California 90012, Tel: (312) 617-3077. Citicorp Plaza, 725 South Figueroa Street, Los Angeles, California 90017, Tel: (213) 626-5433. Fox Hills Mall, 200 Fox Hills Mall, Culver City, California 90230, Tel: (213) 390-7833. Shoreline Village, 407 Shoreline Village Drive, Long Beach, California 90802, Tel: (213) 435-5911. Olvera Street, West 17 Olvera Street, Los Angeles, California 90012, Tel: (213) 687-4344. 1717 Outlet, 1717 South Figueroa Street, Los Angeles, California 90015, Tel: (213) 746-2347. Steve's Ice Cream, 10918 Le Conte, Westwood, California 90024, Tel: 208-1309.

Sports Stadiums: *The Coliseum:* The summer Olympics took place in this stadium in 1932 and 1984. The professional football team, the Los Angeles Raiders, and the college team, the U.S.C. Trojans can be seen here more often. It is located at 3911 Figueroa Street, Tel: (213) 747-7111.

Dodger Stadium: Here, up to 56,000 spectators can watch the Dodgers' home baseball games; 1000 Elysian Park Avenue, Tel: (213) 224-1400.

Forum: From the end of October to the middle of March, this large sports arena is home to the two hockey teams, the Lakers and the Kings. 3900 West Manchester Boulevard in Inglewood, Tel: (213) 674-6000.

Swimming Stadium: This is located directly near the Coliseum. It was the venue of the Olympic swimming competitions. 3966 Menlo Avenue, Tel: (213) 485-2924.

Sport Arena: In this arena, also near the Coliseum, the USC basketball team takes on its opponents. 3939 S. Figueroa St., Tel: (213) 748-6131.

Transportation

Bus: The Southern California Rapid Transit District (RTD) bus system is inexpensive but can be very time consuming. For the entire regions of the city, the RTD has published a brochure with schedules and routes to around 100 attractions. These, along with inexpensive three-day bus passes are available at the RTD Ticket Counter, Level B, Arco Plaza, Fifth and Flower Street; RTD offices are also at 425 South Main Street, and in Hollywood at 6249 Hollywood Boulevard.

Information: Tel: (213) 626-4455.

Greyhound, 208 East Sixth Street, Tel: (213) 620-1200.

Continental Trailways, 800 North Alameda Street, Union Station Building, Tel: (213) 742-1200.

Green Tortoise, Tel: (213) 392-1990.

Taxis: The fares for taxis are about $2 for the first mile and $1.50 for each additional mile.

Trains: Union Station, terminal station for the Amtrak routes, 800 North Alameda Street, Tel: (213) 624-0171.

Important Addresses

Police, Fire, Emergencies: Tel: 911.

The *Traveller's Aid Society* in the Los Angeles International Airport, Tel: (213) 646-2270 or in the Greyhound Bus Terminal, Tel: (213) 625-2501, will be able to help with all types of problems from medical to legal.

Tourist Information Offices: Los Angeles Visitors and Convention Bureau, Arco Plaza, Level B, Sixth and Flowers Street, Tel: (213) 689-8822. Open from Monday to Friday from 8:30 am to 5 pm.

Los Angeles International Airport (LAX), Bradley International Terminal, on the arrival and departure levels, Tel: (213) 215-0606. Open daily from 8:30 am to 9 pm.

Broadway, Hollywood Building, Hollywood and Vine Street, Tel: (213) 628-3101.

Los Angeles Chamber of Commerce, 404 South Bixel Street, Tel: (213) 629-0711.

Chinese Chamber of Commerce, 978 North Broadway, Tel: (213) 617-0396.

Automobile Club of Southern California, 2601 South Figueroa Street, Tel: (213) 741-3111 or (213) 741-4070.

Los Angeles City Recreation and Parks Department, City Hall East, 200 North Main Street, Tel: (213) 485-5555.

Weather Forecast: Tel: (213) 554-1212.

Airport: The Los Angeles International Airport (LAX) is the third largest airport in the world. It is located 17 miles southwest of the downtown area on Century and Sepulveda Boulevards directly on Santa Monica Bay; Tel: (213) 646-5252.

Maps and Informational Materials

Maps and Informational Materials are available free of charge from the Tourist and Information Bureaus, the Visitor Centers and the Chambers of Commerce in individual cities.

Road maps are available from the triple A *(→Automobile Club)* or they can be purchased at service stations.

By contacting the following addresses, one can also request useful information. Some of these organisations do, however, charge a fee. One should also contact these addresses well in advance.

General information on the state of California:

California Office of Tourism, 1121 L Street, Suite 103, Sacramento, California 95814; Tel: (916) 322-1396.

Information on national parks:

National Park Service Information, Fort Mason, Building 201, Bay and Franklin Streets, San Francisco, California 94123; Tel: (415) 556-4122.

Information on state parks and recreation areas:

California State Park System, Department of Parks and Recreation, P.O. Box 2390, Sacramento, California 95811; Tel: (916) 445-6477.

Medical Care

The standards of medicine in California are excellent. Payment for medical and dental treatment is expected immediately in cash or by credit card *(→Money),* making a travel health insurance policy recommendable *(→Health Insurance).*

Most larger cities will have a medical and dental referral service listed in the telephone book. They will be able to recommend general physicians and specialists depending on what treatment is required.

Almost all of the National Parks are equipped with a medical clinic or at least a first aid station.

Mendocino

If driving along the winding coastal road from San Francisco heading north, after a curve, one will see the southern view of the picturesque coastal village of Mendocino, high atop the coastal cliffs on the opposite side of the bay. This town has numerous well preserved buildings from the past century. Especially worth visiting is the Kelly House Historical Museum at 45007 Albion Street. The house itself dates back to the year 1861 and the museum is open daily from 1 to 4 pm. Nearby at 45200 Little Lake Road is a gallery open daily from 10 am to 5 pm.

One should not miss seeing the *Little River* and *Pygmy Forests* on Little River Comptche Road. Due to the high soil acidity, the pine and cypress trees only grow to a height of 28 inches.

Accommodation

Camping: Kravis Mendocino Campground, 1/2 mile south of Mendocino on Comptche-Ukiah Road, 9601 Highway 1, 60 tent and RV sites, maximum length for camping vehicles is 20 feet, open from the beginning of April to the end of October, priced from $12 to $14 for up to six persons, reservations are recommended, Tel: (707) 937-3130.

Mendocino Coast/Manchester Beach KOA Campground, on Highway 1 on Manchester State Beach, 1 mile north of Manchester, $20 to $26 for two persons, additional person $2 to $4, reservations are recommended, Tel: (707) 882-2375.

Russian Gulch State Park, 2 miles north of Mendocino on the coastal road, 30 tent and RV sites, maximum length for camping vehicles is 30 feet, very beautiful location, $10 per site, reservations are recommended, Tel: (707) 937-0497 or (707) 937-5804.

Von Damme State Park, 3 miles from Mendocino on Little River, 74 tent and RV sites, $10 per site, reservations are recommended, Tel: (707) 937-0851 or (707) 937-5804.

Motels: Blackberry Inn, one and two persons from $55 to $110, each additional person $5, 44951 Larkin Road, Tel: (707) 937- 5281.

Hill House Inn, reservations are recommended during the summer months, one and two persons from $65 to $125, each additional person $10, Palette Drive, Tel: (707) 937-0554.

Money

Many foreign visitors find the US dollars confusing because they are all similar in size and colour, the difference only apparent in the printed value and which portrait appears on the front. Those visiting California from foreign countries should exchange money into dollars before leaving since some banks will not exchange foreign currencies, or one must order foreign currencies in advance if changing dollars back.

Traveller's cheques are accepted almost everywhere as cash. Therefore, it is a good idea to bring most of one's travel budget in traveller's cheques since they can be replaced if lost or stolen.

Credit cards are also widely accepted and almost a necessity if planning to rent a car. A credit card will also prove handy if one unexpectedly needs to pay larger sums for medical care. Visa and Mastercard (Eurocard/Access) are more widely accepted than American Express and they are accepted in most banks, whereas for American Express, one must go specifically to an American Express office, which might not always be conveniently located.

Monterey

The city of Monterey, located on a beautiful bay and with a population of about 28,000, is historically significant in many respects. Monterey was the capital of Alta California under Spanish, Mexican and American rule. The first stop for any visitor to Monterey should be at the Chamber of Commerce in the Jacinto Rodriguez Adobe, built in 1849 and located on Alvarado Street. Informational materials and free maps are available here. One can also request information on current events.

Those who would like more in-depth information on the interesting history of Monterey should take the three mile long *Path of History,* which can be easily recognised by the red arrows. Along this path, leading predominantly through Old Monterey, are a total of 45 historically significant and architecturally interesting buildings. Some of these buildings can be toured on one's own, others offer guided tours.

One will meet up with numerous tourists on a stroll through Monterey's *Fisherman's Wharf,* which does not reach the dimensions of San Francisco's, but which is just as lively with its exclusive galleries and inevitable souvenir shops as well as excellent restaurants.

Those who travel to Monterey should by no means miss *Cannery Row* - an area which takes full financial advantage of its literary fame. Today, however, Cannery Row differs greatly from its presentation in the novel by John Steinbeck (1902-1968), who was awarded the Nobel Prize for literature in 1962. The canneries described in his famous book, which processed sardines, had to close in the mid 1940's when the sardines were no longer caught off the coast. After this, the entire district fell into decay and sank into oblivion up until the time when Steinbeck wrote "Cannery Row" *(→Literature)* in 1945. In this novel, he describes the life of the residents here as a colourful composite of vagabonds, drunks, prostitutes and labourers, not only bringing this part of Monterey world fame, but reanimating it as well. Today, most of the antiques shops, art galleries, restaurants and, of course, souvenir shops can be found in this area. Cannery Row can, however, no longer be compared to that described by Steinbeck. One of the few buildings that has remained intact is at 851 Cannery Row, near to the Monterey Bay Aquarium. For Steinbeck, "Kalisa's" was a bordello; today, it is a quaint little restaurant and café. Friday and Saturday evenings, there is often live entertainment, Tel: (408) 372-8512.

The Monterey Bay Aquarium at 886 Cannery Row is one of the largest saltwater aquariums in the world, making it among the most interesting attractions in this city.

The Aquarium is open daily from, 10 am to 6 pm. Admission is $8 for adults, $3.50 for children from 3 to 12 and $5.50 for students; Information: Tel: (408) 646-3866.

The Monterey cypress trees are just beautiful as they are rare ▶

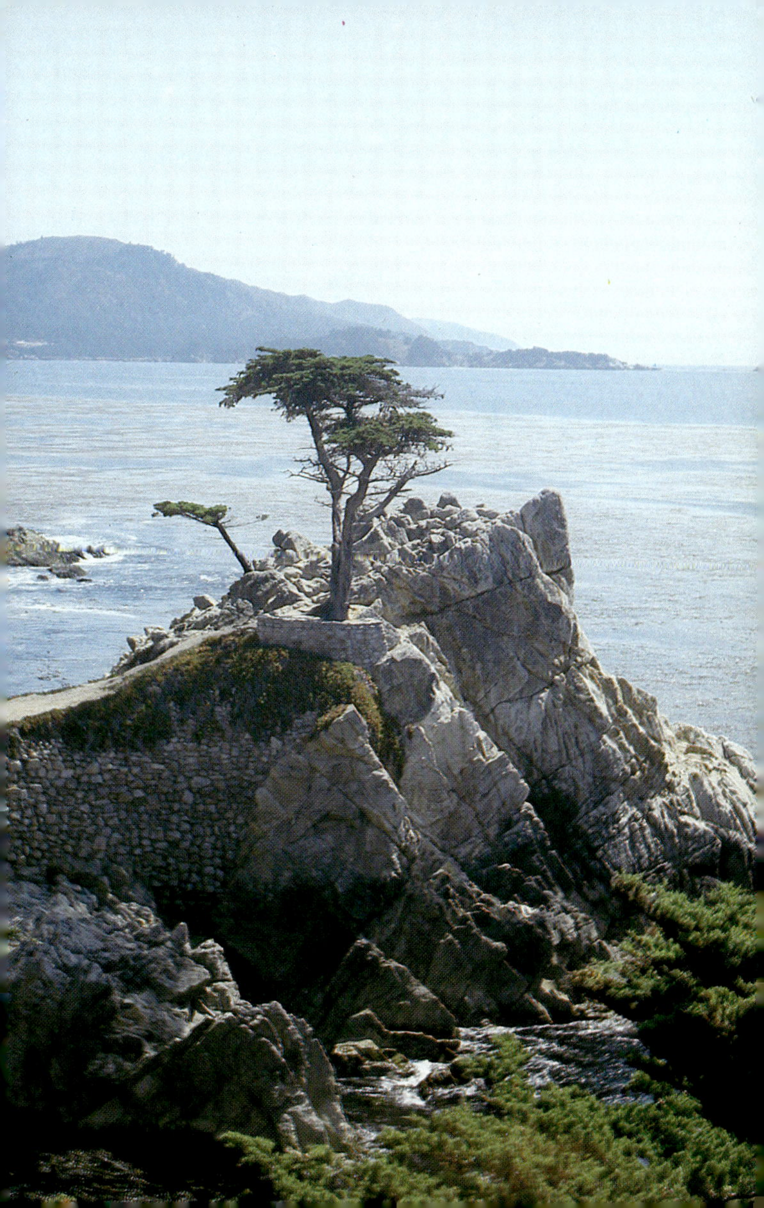

Monterey / Practical Information

John Steinbeck's *Cannery Row* is definitely recommended reading before visiting the Monterey area.

The *Monterey Peninsula Airport* lies in the direction of Salinas, not far from the center of town.

The *Greyhound Station* is near the wharf on Del Monte Boulevard. The trip to San Francisco lasts around 3½ hours. The local bus lines, the Monterey Peninsula Transit, organises trips to all of the significant, beautiful and interesting attractions in this area, for example Pacific Grove, Carmel and Big Sur.

For fishing enthusiasts: *fishing trips* are offered, departing from the harbour. During the whale migration from December to March, boats depart from Fisherman's Wharf in Monterey at 9 am and 1 pm to offer a view up close. These trips last between 1½ and 2 hours. Information is available and reservations can be made by contacting: Monterey Sport Fishing, 96 Old Fisherman's Wharf 1, Monterey, California 93940, Tel: (408) 372-2203.

Every year in September, the world famous jazz festival takes place in Monterey, lasting several days.

Information: Monterey Peninsula Chamber of Commerce and Visitors and Convention Bureau, P.O. Box 1770, Monterey, California 93940, Tel: (408) 649-3200.

Accommodation

Camping: Carmel Valley-Riverside RV Park, 35 RV sites, about 4½ miles on Carmel Valley Road after turning off Highway 1, then about 1¼ miles on Shuttle Road, priced from $20 per person, additional persons $2 each, reservations are recommended, Tel: (408) 624-9329.

Motels: Best Western De Anza Inn, $50 to $75 for one and two persons, additional person $6, 2141 Fremont Street, Tel: (408) 646-8300.

Carmel Motor Hill Lodge, $70 for one and two persons, additional person $6, reservations are required, 1374 Munras Avenue, Tel: (408) 373-3252.

Comfort Inn, priced from $45 for one and two persons, additional person $3, reservations are required, 2050 Fremont Street, Tel: (408) 373-3081 or 1-800-228-5150.

Franciscan Inn, priced from $50 for one and two persons, additional person $5, reservations are required, 2058 Fremont Street, Tel: (408) 375-9511.
Montero Lodge, $35 to $70 for one and two persons depending on the season, additional person $5, reservations are required, 1240 Munras Avenue, Tel: (408) 375-6002.
Scottish Fairway Motel, priced from $40 to $70 for one and two persons depending on the season, additional person $6, reservations required, 2075 Fremont Street, Tel: (408) 373-5551.
Sixpence Inn, $35 to $60 for one and two persons, additional person $6, reservations are recommended, 100 Reservation Road, Tel: (408) 384-1000.
YMCA: Monterey Peninsula YMCA Hostel, open from June 20 to August 20, $8 for members, $9 for non-members, 404 Camino El Estero, advance notice of arrival is necessary, Tel: (408) 373-4166.

Muir Woods National Monument

Muir Woods National Monument covers an area of about 500 acres with beautiful redwood groves, which are very inviting for a long stroll. There are no roadways through the monument, but there are well marked hiking trails, totalling over 6 miles in length. At the entrance to the monument (open from 8 am until dusk) one can obtain a pamphlet with a description of the area including the hiking trails. Admission is free of charge. One can reach the Muir Woods National Monument by driving from San Francisco over the Golden Gate Bridge and continuing 17 miles along State Highway 1 heading northwest.
Park Address: Superintendent, Muir Woods National Monument, Mill Valley, California 94941, Tel: (415) 388-2595.

Napa Valley

Napa Valley, located a little over an hour north of San Francisco, is known as the "Disneyland of Wine." This region is the Mecca of wine connoisseurs. The valley winds through a landscape of rolling hills along the Napa stream toward San Pablo Bay. Highway 29 leads 35 miles through the wine country and is considered the American wine route. This region has an ideal climate for the grapes to ripen: sunshine (but not too much sunshine as is the case in Southern California) with cool nights and morning fog from the bay; ample rain in autumn and winter. Sweetening the wine is prohibited, but this would also be superfluous; adding acidity is permitted.

The wine town of Yountville can trace its name back to George Yount, the man who planted the first grapevines in the valley in 1838. Napa Valley gained an unexpected renowned only in the past few years. Whitewashed manor houses from the era of Spanish rule, the famous Rhine House owned by the Behringer Family and the French châteaus like the one in the famous Beaulieu Vineyards are popular destinations for the increasing tourism. A total of around 40 wine cellars offer tours and wine tastings to attract visitors. Among these are, for example, the Behringer Vineyards near Saint Helena and the Mondavi Winery about 18 miles north of Oakville, built in the Spanish mission style of architecture.

Nature Reserves

Nature reserves, especially the national and state parks, are among the main tourist attractions in the United States. The Grand Canyon is only one example.

The national parks are administrated by the National Park Service, a division of the Department of the Interior. The smaller and often just as beautiful State Parks fall under the administration of the individual states. Within the national parks, any private use or change in the natural condition of the park is prohibited. This includes any construction for commercial purposes other than those covered by the concessions awarded by the National Park Service in regard to forestry, hunting, water rights etc. Even airlines are not permitted to fly over national parks.

Due to these strict regulations which protect these areas, the wildlife is very trusting, not having learned to fear humans. Animals quite often approach visitors without any shyness. The parks are not bordered by fences; thus, the freedom of movement of the wildlife is not restricted in any way. The only noticeable borders are marked by signs along the roadways at the entrances to the parks.

The landscapes in Yosemite National Park are some of the most beautiful that California has to offer ▶

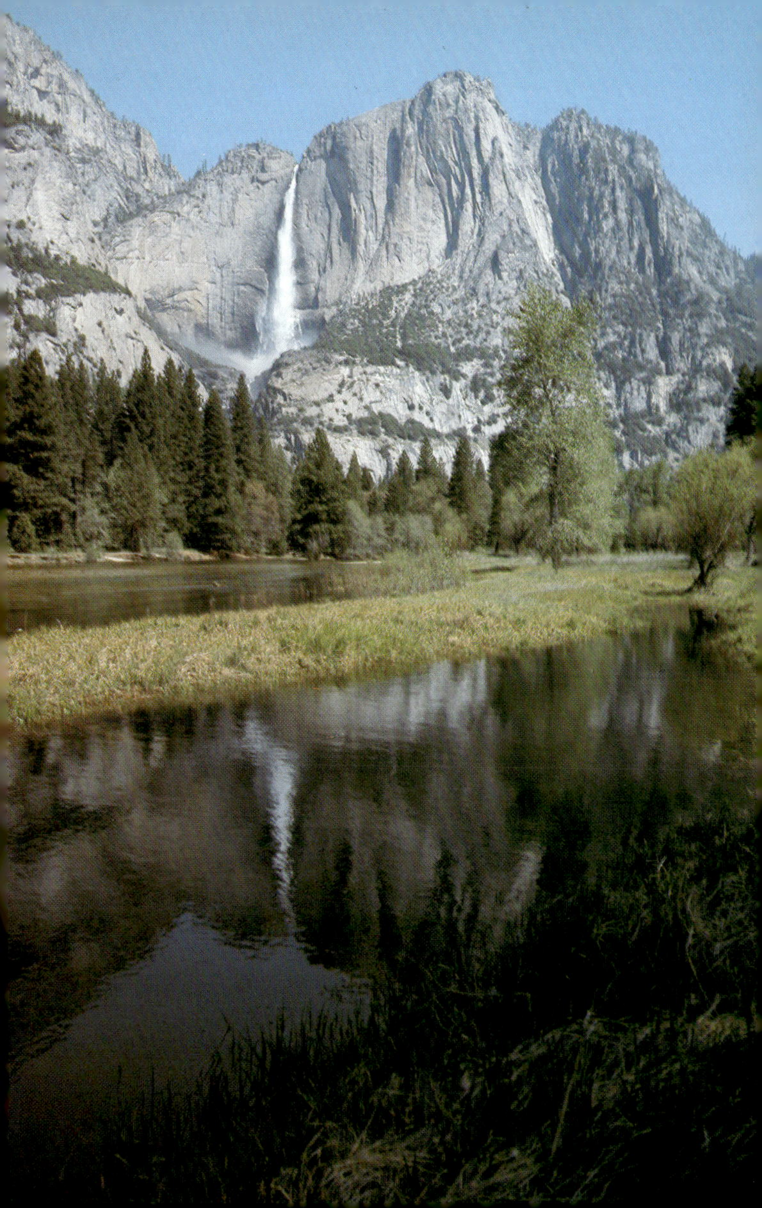

At the booths at the entrances to the parks, an admission fee of $5 per vehicle is charged. Those who plan to visit at least five of these parks should buy the "Golden Eagle Passport" for $25 which is valid for all of the parks belonging to the National Park System for one year. Seniors can obtain the "Golden Age Passport" which is valid for free admission to all of the parks and includes reduced rates at the campsites run by the parks.

The roadways within the California nature reserves are in good condition. In the most well known national parks, there are a generous portion of parking areas at observation points; however, these are not always sufficient to accommodate the number of visitors with camping and recreational vehicles. Therefore, it is a good idea to start a tour of a given park early in the morning. Quite often, there are picnic tables, benches, grill areas etc. at these areas. Attempting to camp out overnight here is prevented by the park rangers.

The extensive system of hiking trails covers even the most remote regions of the parks. Hiking and backpacking have meanwhile become one of the most popular activities in the parks. If one obtains a "backcountry permit," the necessary permit for hiking tours combined with camping, one can hike from one backcountry campsite to the next for several days. For shorter hikes or only strolls through the landscape, one should choose the educational self-guiding trails, where interesting information is given either on signs or a brochure on the history, geology, inhabitants, wildlife and flora of the park.

The friendly park rangers in the brown uniforms are employees of the federal government, and view themselves not only as protectors of nature but are also willing to answer any questions and help visitors in any way they can. At certain times posted in the visitor centers or at the campsites, a diverse programme is offered free of charge. These ranger-led activities range from slide shows and films to lectures at sites of natural interest or an evening bonfire lasting several hours to hikes lasting several days. Courses in canoeing, fishing and photography and even animal watching excursions are also offered in many parks. The National Park Service operates the visitor centers, in which excellent informational material and hiking maps are available. In addition, books can be purchased. The

National Park Service is also responsible for the ranger stations and, as a rule, the campsites located within the park.

Practical Information

Information on campsite capacity and vacancies is often posted at the entrances to the parks.

Lodges, cottages, cabins, souvenir shops, and tour organisers in the parks operate on a concession basis. Depending on level of comfort, furnishings and the national park, one must expect to pay around $20 to $50 per night for one or two persons in the accommodations. Almost all of the visitors centers are equipped with restrooms, a room for slide shows and lectures, an information desk and space for exhibitions.

The times quoted for the length of hiking tours through the national parks are often longer than it might take if one is used to hiking at a relatively brisk pace — a tip which might be useful when planning further travel through the state.

Informational material on national parks can be obtained by contacting: Public Information Officer, National Park Service, US Department of the Interior, 1100 Ohio Drive Southwest, Washington DC 20242.

Western Regional Information Office, National Park Service, Fort Mason, Building 201, San Francisco, California 94123; Tel: (415) 556-4122 or (415) 556-0560.

One can also contact each individual national park. The addresses for these can be found under the individual entries in this book.

Pacific Grove

Pacific Grove lies in the northwestern portion of the Monterey Peninsula, about 3 miles from Monterey via Lighthouse Avenue. At the end of this road, one will see the Point Pines Lighthouse. Built in 1855 before the city of Pacific Grove was founded at the end of the 19th century, it still serves its original purpose today. In the interior of the lighthouse is a small nautical museum, which is, however, only open 1 pm to 4 pm from the beginning of January to the end of November. Admission is free of charge, Tel: (408) 372 4212.

Another museum, the Museum of Natural History, can be found at 165 Forest Avenue, directly across from the Pacific Grove Chamber of Commerce. Here, one will find information on a natural spectacle which occurs from the end of October to March and has taken place for as long as can be remembered. During this time, millions of the orange and black monarch butterflies come to Pacific Grove from distant Canada to spend the winter in the *Butterfly Trees* on Ridge Road. The museum is open all year from Tuesday to Sunday from 10 am to 5 pm. Admission is free of charge, Tel: (408) 372-4212.

Accommodation

Best Western Butterfly Trees Lodge, $70 to $90 for one and two persons, additional person $8, 1150 Lighthouse Avenue, Tel: (408) 372-0503.

Olympia Motor Lodge, $50 to $80 for one and two persons, additional person $10, 3665 Rio Road, Tel: (408) 624-1841.

People

"California — the Golden State": this description is true for many aspects of this state. This is not only true of the gold rush era and not only of the cities; it describes not only the natural landscapes in this state, but the people as well. Now as ever, they swarm to California, mainly tourists but still immigrants, predominantly from Mexico, but also from the Philippines, England and Canada. This is a major reason for the cultural diversity and possibly for the tolerant attitudes and high level of mobility.

California is, with a population of almost 24 million residents, the most heavily populated state in the union, with one fourth of the population having been born in a foreign country.

About 25% of the total population is made up of various racial minorities. The Anglo-Saxons comprise the largest proportion with 76%. According to the last census in 1980, 4.6 million people are of Mexican descent, making them the largest minority. Almost half live in the greater Los Angeles area. Blacks make up the second largest minority with 1.8 million, making up 7.7% of the population.

Japanese (220,000), Chinese (170,000) and Filipinos (140,000) are the most widely represented of the 1.2 million Asians to have settles in the large metropolitan areas of Los Angeles, San Francisco and Fresno.

The original and actual lords over this land meanwhile see themselves as having been austed, now the smallest minority: the Native Americans.

They make up only 0.9% of the total population or about 200,000. Most Native Americans live in and around San Francisco, Los Angeles and San Diego. The fewest of them have remained on the reservations near San Diego, Fresno and Eureka.

Due to the size of the Spanish speaking minority, a culture within a culture has developed in Los Angeles. Many of the signs in Los Angeles are in English and Spanish. Meanwhile, 50 local television stations broadcast in English and Spanish and there are over 200 radio stations in the United States broadcasting only in Spanish.

Of course, the other "minority" of California could be considered the "beautiful people." From the cream of the crop in the film industry to the wealthy and politically influential.

Photography

California is a paradise for photographers — amateur and professional alike. Film is available everywhere in California. One should, however, protect film from the Californian heat. A good place for it is in a refrigerator or on the air conditioning unit in a hotel. This will extend the life of the film. It is also best to have the film developed in the same general area it was purchased since there could be differences in colour.

Pismo Beach

At Pismo Beach on Highway 1, only a few miles south of San Luis Obispo, the residents are very proud of their beach — the only beach in California allowing motorised vehicles. For this reason the beach tends to be quite lively and colourful during summer weekends, when hobbyists from the surrounding areas try out their home-made vehicles, dune buggies and three-wheeled beach motorcycles. The rental fee for such a beach motorcycle starts at around $50 per hour.

Accommodation

La Sage Riviera Campground, 87 RV sites, $14 to $16 for one and two persons, additional person $1, 319 Highway 1, reservations are recommended, Tel: (805) 489-2103 or (805) 489-5506.

Pismo Coast Village Campground, 400 RV sites, reservations are recommended, $16 to $25 depending on the season for up to six persons, additional guests $1 each, 165 South Dolliver Street, Tel: (805) 773-1811. Pismo State Beach, 185 tent and RV sites, $10 to $14 for up to eight persons, located near the Pismo Coast Village Campground, Tel: (805) 489-2684.

Point Reyes National Seashore

Near Olema, almost 45 miles northwest of San Francisco, the coastal road branches off into an extensive landscape of sand dunes and lagoons, covering an area of over 100 square miles. The Point Reyes National Seashore includes a long peninsula, which can — excepting the roadway — be explored in its entire length of 100 miles on foot, horseback or by bicycle. Before reaching the outermost point, *Point Reyes,* the sea lions have declared the area their playground. In addition, this is considered an especially favourable vantage point for observing the migration of the whales. The generously laid out *Bear Valley Visitor Canter* and park headquarters, around $1/2$ mile west of Olema, offers all of the necessary information, useful maps as well as an interesting film show. It is open during the entire year. In addition, within the park are also Point Reyes Light Visitor Center, open from Thursday to Monday, and the Drakes Beach Visitor Center, open weekends. The latter was so named because Sir Francis Drake is said to have landed there.

Point Reyes National Seashore / Practical Information
Accommodation
Camping: The four camping sites on Point Reyes National Seashore are equipped with grills, picnic tables, laundry facilities, but do not have showers. A camping permit is required; this can be obtained at the park headquarters. During the summer, reservations are recommended. All of the sites are open all year and can be used free of charge. They are, however, only accessible on foot. Tel: (415) 663-1092.
Sky Camp, 12 sites, on the western slope of the 980 foot Mount Wittenberg, about a 3 mile hike from the headquarters.
Wildcat Camp, 12 sites, near Wildcat Beach, $6 1/4$ mile hike from the headquarters.

Coast Camp, 14 sites, about 220 yards from the beach, 8 mile hike from the headquarters.

Glen Camp, 12 sites, in a small, wooded valley, about 4½ mile hike from the headquarters.

Youth Hostel: Point Reyes Hostel, $8 for members, reservations are required during the summer, southwest of the park headquarters on Limantour Road.

Address: Point Reyes Hostel, P.O. Box 247, Point Reyes Station, CA 94956, Tel: (415) 669-7414.

Restaurants: The small town of Inverness, northwest of the park headquarters, is a good tip for excellent food, especially oysters.

Important Addresses

Park Headquarters: Superintendent, Point Reyes National Seashore, Point Reyes, CA 94956, Tel: (415) 663-1092.

Police

The California Police are very helpful and friendly toward visitors, which is quite a crass contrast to the picture painted of them in films and on television.

Municipal police cars are green and white, while the California Highway Patrol cars are black and white. Speed limits are strictly enforced and violations can be quite expensive →*(Speed Limits)*.

The police can be reached by phoning the emergency number 911.

Politics

The capital of the state of California has been Sacramento since 1854. It serves as an administrative centre and simultaneously provides a balance to the massive metropolitan areas along the coast — a certain political buffer.

The role of the Governor of California is a very powerful one, due to the geographical size and population of the state. The Governor and 40 senators are elected every four years. California also has an "Assembly" with 80 representatives elected every two years. California joined the union in 1849. In 1879, the original constitution was replaced with a second version, one of the longest constitutions in the world. Meanwhile, the constitution of California has over 350 amendments.

The executive branch of the California government is comprised of the governor and six executive officials. The Lieutenant Governor is the second in command and simultaneously the speaker of the Senate. The Secretary of State, in addition to other responsibilities, oversees the elections. The State Attorney General is in charge of the judicial branch and the Treasurer and Controller are responsible for economy and finance. Finally, there is the Superintendent of Public Education, responsible for the education sector.

California is divided politically into 58 counties.

California also plays an important role in national politics due to its size, economic importance and large population. With a total of 45 Representatives to the House, they claim over 10 per cent of the total seats.

Postal System

Generally speaking, post offices are open from Monday to Friday from 8 am to 5 or 6 pm depending on the local business hours; Saturdays, from 8 am to noon and are closed Sundays and holidays. In some of the large metropolitan areas, post offices offer 24 hour service.

For those sending overseas letters, these usually take 5 to 10 days to reach their destinations. Overseas letters cost 45 cents, post cards, 36 cents; within the United States, postcards cost 15 cents and letters cost 25 cents. Postage stamps are available at post offices, in many hotels, airports and even some supermarkets. In addition, there are some postage stamp vending machines, but these charge around 10% more than the value of the stamps.

Visitors to California can have letters and parcels shipped to them by general delivery. The addresses for Los Angeles and San Francisco are then as follows: Mr./Mrs. XYZ, c/o General Delivery, Metropolitan Station, 901 South Broadway, Los Angeles, California 90014; and Mr./Mrs. XYZ, c/o General Delivery, Main Post Office, 7th and Mission Street, San Francisco, California 94101.

The Golden State — the land of the wealthy and the beautiful ▶

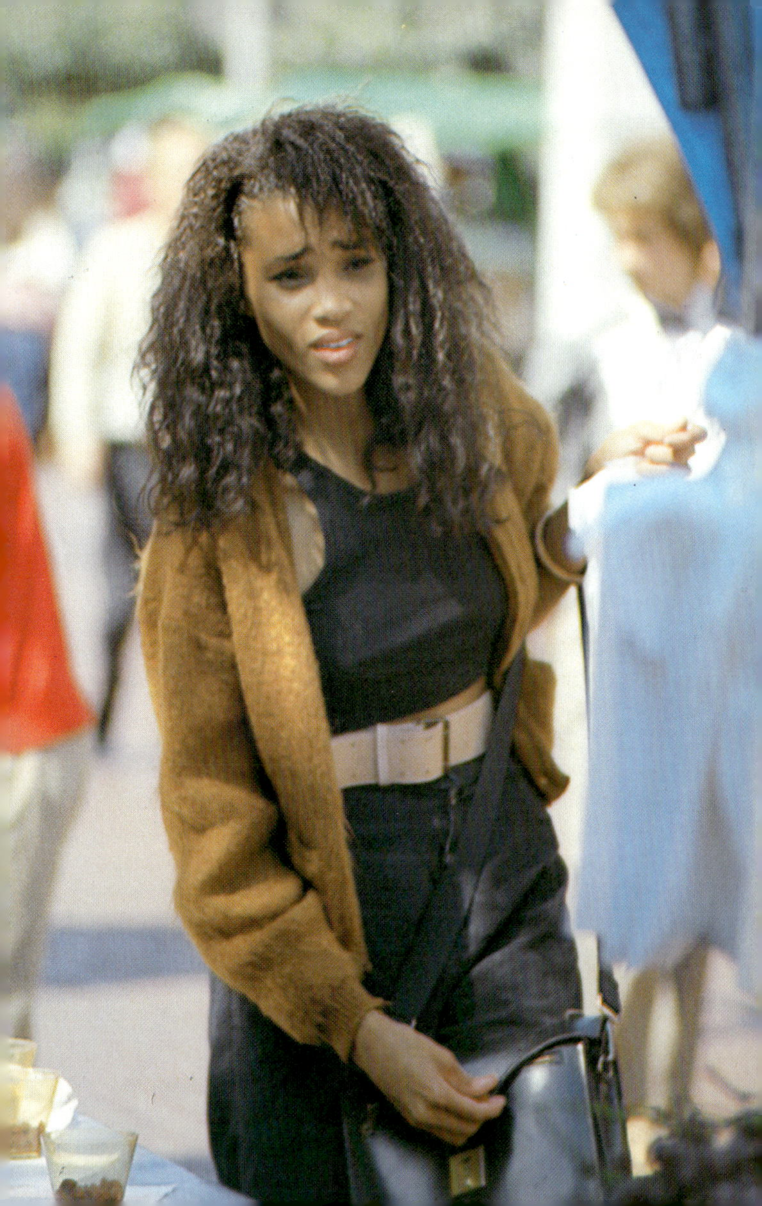

General delivery letters must be claimed within 30 days of their arrival. One must present a valid form of identification like a driving licence or passport.

Private Accommodation →*Accommodation*
Public Transportation →*Travel in California*

Redwood National Park

The Redwood National Park, covering an area of 165 square miles, is a narrow, 40 mile long strip of coastline along the Pacific in the northwestern portion of California. US 101 leads through this landscape and connects the two towns at the entrances on the opposite ends of the park, *Orick* to the south and *Crescent City* to the north.

Redwood National Park was first declared a nature reserve in 1968 and is among the most beautiful regions dominated by the up to 2,000 year old trees.

Near Orick is the *Lady Bird Johnson Grove* and the magnificent 9 mile long *Redwood Creek Trail* leading to *Tall Tree Grove.* The over 600 year old *Libbey Tree* is said to be the largest tree in the world, with a height of 367 feet.

A shuttle bus departs from the ranger station and information center in Orick to this area. The price for the bus trip is $3 for adults and $1 for children, Tel: (707) 488-3461.

East of Crescent City is the *Stout Grove,* in which the most beautiful group of giant sequoias grow.

The trip along Davison Road on the Gold Bluffs Beach to Fern Canyon offers an impressive contrast to the mammoth trees. The road branches off from the US 101 about 2 miles south of Orick. Along the Pacific coast is also the 8 mile long Coastal Drive south of Klamath. From here, one can observe the migration of the whales from December to March. In addition, a large number of sea lions and seals can be found along this section of coastline.

A tour of a sawmill is offered near Orick at the entrance to the Lady Bird Johnson Grove.

Park Address: Superintendent, Redwood National Park, 1111 Second Street, Crescent City, California 95531, Tel: (707) 464-6101.

The headquarters with a visitor center is located in Crescent City. In addition there is a smaller visitor center in Hiouchi and in Orick.

Restaurants

California has restaurants to suit just about every taste and budget, from coffee shops, truck stops and fast food restaurants to exclusive restaurants which rank among the best in the world. One will find the ethnic diversity of this state reflected in the selection of restaurants, with ethnic specialties available from around the world and often served in an authentic atmosphere.

In most of the restaurants in the middle and upper price categories, it is often recommended or even necessary to make reservations. The prices for restaurants can vary greatly, not only depending on the restaurant itself, but on the location as well. To offer an orientation, breakfast ranges from $2 to $8; lunch from $8 to $16; and dinners start at around $10.

San Diego

The history of California begins with San Diego, the oldest city in this state. In 1542, Juan Rodriguez Cabrillo landed at Point Loma, discovered this section of land and laid claim on it for the Spanish crown. However, a permanent settlement was first established in the year 1769, together with the first of the twenty-one Catholic missions in California. Gaspar de Portola and Junipero Serra were the founding fathers of this settlement. The ensuing events would prove turbulent. The history of this region is characterised by a mix of the Mexican, Spanish and American cultures, which will be perceived by any visitor during a stroll through this city at every step along the way. The historical origins can best be traced in *Old Town* in San Diego. The marked cultural diversity, the geographical location in close proximity to Mexico, its pleasant climatic conditions and its lush vegetation make San Diego a preferred holiday destination in the southern regions of California. At present, San Diego has about one million residents; when including the surrounding metropolitan area, it is about two million, making it the second largest city in California.

San Diego / Sights

Balboa Park: This 1,160 acre park complex northeast of the downtown area counts among the most beautiful areas in the city. Even before the turn of the century, the resident of San Diego used this area as a city park up until 1915 and 1916, when it became the site of the Panama-California Exposition, advancing it to the status of point of interest, even for the residents of San Diego. With the beginning of this exposition, the park retained its original name, having been named after the Spanish explorer and navigator Nuñez de Balboa (1475-1517), who, among other accomplishments, crossed the Central American regions to South America.

In addition to a number of museums built in Spanish-Moorish architecture, Balboa Park is also home to the famous *San Diego Zoo* and the *Botanical Building,* housed in a former Victorian Train Station for the Santa Fe Railway. The zoo is one of the largest in the world and is one of San Diego's most popular attractions. During the season, it is open daily from 8:30 am to 6:30 pm. Admission for adults is $8.50, children under 16 $3.50, Tel: (619) 231-1515. Deluxe Tour (admission, bus tour, Children's Zoo) adults $12, children from 3 to 15, $6.

Aerospace Historical Center: Within this complex are the Aerospace Museum and the Aerospace Hall of Fame. Among other exhibitions, one can see the legendary "Spirit of Saint Louis," with which Charles Lindbergh became the first to succeed in flying across the Atlantic in 1927. The center is open daily from 10 am to 4:30 pm, admission: adults $3.50, visitors under 18 years of age pay $1. Admission is free of charge every first Tuesday of each month.

Aerospace Museum, 2001 Pan American Plaza, Balboa Park, San Diego, California 92101, Tel: (619) 234-8291.

Natural History Museum, P.O. Box 1390, Balboa Park, San Diego, California 92112, Tel: (619) 232-3821.

Open daily from 10 am to 4:30 pm. Admission for adults is $3, for visitors under 18, $1. Admission is free of charge every first Tuesday of each month.

Old Globe Theatre: This theatre can look back on a long and successful history. Its large uncovered stage is the showplace for the San Diego Shakespeare Festival from the middle of June to September.

Old Globe Theatre, Simon Edison Centre for the Performing Arts, P.O. Box 2171, San Diego, California 92112, Tel: (619) 231-1941.

Reuben H. Fleet Space Theater and Science Center: The most popular shows in this planetarium is the simulation of various space flights, films about the NASA aerospace programme and laser light shows.

The center is open Sundays to Thursdays from 9:45 to 9:30 and Fridays and Saturdays from 9:45 to 10:30.

Admission to the Space Theater: Adults $4.50, visitors under 16 years of age, $3. Admission to the Science Center: free of charge with a Space Theater ticket, otherwise adults pay $2 and children under 16 pay 75 cents. Tel: (619) 238-1168.

San Diego Museum of Art: The collection includes, among others, works by Rembrandt, Giotto, Rubens, Bouguereau, Picasso, O'Keefe, Degas, Munch, Monet, Rodin, Moore and Calder.

Home to the Panama-California Exposition in 1915 and 1916, Balboa Park was named after the Spanish seafarer Nuñez de Balboa

The Museum of Art is open from Tuesday to Sunday from 10 am to 5 pm. Admission: $5 for adults, $2 for visitors from 13 to 18 years of age as well as students, $1 for children from 6 to 12 years of age.

San Diego Museum of Art, P.O. Box 2107, San Diego, California 92112, Tel: (619) 231-7931.

San Diego Museum of Man: This anthropological museum is focussed on the local history of the Native American cultures and the Mayan culture. The Museum of Man is open daily from 10 am to 4:30 pm. Admission: $2 for adults, students and visitors up to the age of 17 pay 75 cents.

San Diego Museum of Man, 1350 El Prado, Balboa Park, San Diego, California 92101, Tel: (619) 239-2001.

Spreckels Organ Pavillion: Free organ concerts on Sundays at 2 pm, Tel: (619) 236-5717.

Timken Art Gallery: This gallery houses paintings by European and American artists as well as an exhibition of Russian icons.

Timken Art Gallery is open from Tuesday to Saturday from 10 am to 4:30 pm, Sundays from 1:30 to 4:30 pm.

Timken Art Gallery, 1500 El Prado, Balboa Park, San Diego, California 92101, Tel: (619) 239-5548.

Downtown Area: The downtown area of San Diego is an ideal starting point for a tour of this city. The Visitors Information Center *(→Important Addresses under Practical Information),* the old, well restored Amtrak Station and the Greyhound and Trailways terminals are all located in this area. From downtown, municipal buses depart for all the major attractions and points of interest. The attractions within the downtown area are all quite concentrated and it is easy to find good hotels and motels in this area.

Gaslamp Quarter: This district of San Diego borders the downtown area to the south and remained the hub of the city up until the turn of the century. Gradually, however, the flair of this district paled as did the facades of the buildings which only appeared beautiful and worth preserving to those with a trained eye. After extensive renovations, these Victorian houses were given back their former lustre and newly opened galleries, stylish restaurants and a number of other shops and boutiques are proof of a growing public interest in this area. The section of Fifth Avenue especially has a character all its own.

The Gaslamp Quarter Council organises free tours from its offices at 652 Fifth Avenue on Fridays from noon to 1 pm and Saturdays from 10 am to noon and from 1 to 3 pm, Tel: (619) 233-5227.

Maritime Museum: The windjammer "Star of India," a trading vessel built in 1863 on the Isle of Man in the Irish Sea between England and Ireland; the ferry "Berkeley" from the year 1898, which operated in the waters of the San Francisco Bay area; and the steamship "Medea" from 1904 can be seen here daily from 9 am to 8 pm.

Admission for adults is $5, visitors between 13 and 17 years of age pay $3, and children between 6 and 12 are charged $1.

Maritime Museum Association of San Diego, 1306 North Harbor Drive, San Diego, California 92101, Tel: (619) 234-9153.

Seaport Village: This shopping district has the atmosphere and character of an old fishing village.

Seaport Village, 849 West Harbor Drive, San Diego, California 92101, Tel: (619) 235-4014.

La Jolla: This district, located in the northern part of San Diego is famous for its beaches and bays, its coastal rock formations and sandstone cliffs, with bizarrely shaped caves and its pleasant atmosphere. This district is the home of the University of California at San Diego (UCSD).

La Jolla Museum of Contemporary Art: This museum exhibits works by contemporary artists including Warhol and Lichtenstein, Anuszkiewicz and Kelly, Ryman and Judd as well as the packaging artist Christo, who drew attention all over the world with his umbrellas between Japan and California in the summer of 1991.

The museum is open from Tuesday to Friday from 10 am to 5 pm, Saturdays and Sundays from 10 am to 5 pm; admission for adults is $3, students pay $1.50 and children under 12 pay 50 cents.

La Jolla Museum of Contemporary Art, 700 Prospect Street, La Jolla, California 92037, Tel: (619) 454-0261.

Mission Bay Park: This district was once swampland and has been in the process of being transformed into an extensive recreation area for years. Measured in terms of the number of visitors, this area has the largest attractions in San Diego.

Sea World: This park with aquatic shows attracts visitors with a total of eight performances by dolphins, sea lions, and several killer whales. During the summer, Sea World offers a spectacular show during the evenings. Sea World is open during the summer from 9 am to 11 pm and during the remainder of the year from 9 am to dusk. Admission is $25 for adults and $16 for children from 3 to 11 years of age.

Sea World, 1720 South Shores Road, San Diego, California 92109, Tel: (619) 226-3901.

Old Town: This is the location of the first mission in California, a military fortress and later the first settlement in California. The old buildings have been in part restored and rebuilt. Along with lovely shops and several good restaurants, these make up a State Historic Park. Information on guided tours and other special events is available by contacting:

Old Town State Park, 2645 San Diego Avenue, San Diego, California 92110, Tel: (619) 237-6770.

Point Loma: This is the name of the small peninsula between the city of San Diego and the Pacific Ocean. The *Cabrillo Monument* was built in honour of Juan Rodriguez Cabrillo, who went ashore here in 1542. The visitor center is open daily from 10 am to 4 pm. Tel: (619) 293-5450.

Behind the over 130 year old lighthouse is a *whale overlook,* from which one can observe the annual migration of the whales. It also offers a beautiful panorama. In the visitor center there is an exhibition as well as a film presentation offering interesting background information on the whales.

Whale Watching: San Diego is the ideal point to observe the migration of the Californian grey whales from December to March from Point Loma or other sections of the coast. It is even better to take a tour by boat which will offer an even closer view of the whales.

Invader Cruise, 1066 North Harbour Drive, Tel: (619) 234-8687 or 1-800-262-4386 in California and 1-800-445-4386 within the United States. The $3^{1}/_{2}$ hour tours start Tuesdays to Sundays at 9:30 am and 1:30 pm.

San Diego / Practical Information
Accommodation
Camping: Border Gate RV Park, 179 RV sites, 2 persons $20, additional person $2, 4141 San Ysidro Boulevard, Tel: (619) 428-4411.

Campland on the Bay, 682 tent and RV sites, $18-38 for five persons, additional person $4, 2211 Pacific Beach Drive, Tel: (619) 274-6260.

Chula Vista RV Park, 240 RV sites, $32 for two persons, additional person $2, 460 Sandpiper Way, Tel: (619) 422-0111.

De Anza Harbor Resort, 250 RV sites, $18-32 for four persons, additional person $3, 2727 De Anza Road, Tel: (619) 273-3211.

San Diego Metro KOA, tent and RV sites, $23-29 for two persons, additional person $2-3, 111 North Second Avenue in Chula Vista, reservations are recommended, Tel: (619) 427-3601.

Hotels/Motels: Bay View Inn, $50-70 one and two persons, additional person $5, 4610 De Soto Street, Tel: (619) 483-9800 and 1-800-542-6010.

Best Western Airport Inn, $45-60 one and two persons, additional person $7, 2901 Nimitz Boulevard, Tel: (619) 224-3655.

The Best Western chain has 12 additional hotels in San Diego.

Circle 8 Motor Inn, $50-70 one and two persons, additional person $6, 543 Hotel Circle South, Tel: (619) 297-8800 and 1-800-227-4734.

Executive Lodge, $45-55 one and two persons, additional person $4, 5415 Clairemont Mesa Boulevard, Tel: (619) 560-0545 and 1-800-854-6111.

Youth Hostel/YMCA: Point Loma Hostel, $9 for members, 3790 Udall Street, Tel: (619) 223-4778.

Imperial Beach Hostel, $9 for members, 170 Palm Avenue, near the Mexican border, Tel: (619) 423-8039.

YMCA, $16-24 for one and two persons, 1115 East Eighth Avenue, Tel: (619) 232-7451.

San Diego Armed Service YMCA Hostel, $9 for members, 500 West Broadway, Tel: (619) 232-1113.

Car Rental: In addition to the widely known agencies, there are several which have significantly lower prices. These include:

Amcoe Rent A Car, 1320 Broadway, Tel: (619) 238-1305;

Cheap Heaps Rent A Car, 904 West Grape Street, Tel: (619) 231-5719 or 811 25th Street, Tel: (619) 235-8733;

Rent A Wreck, 4550 La Jolla Boulevard, Tel: (619) 551-0203 or 1-800-243-3523.

Some agencies prohibit driving rental cars into Mexico. One should, therefore, ask about this condition before signing the rental contract.

Medical Care: Medical Society Referral Service, Tel: (619) 565-8161 (for general consultation).

Dental Society Referral Service, Tel: (619) 223-5391 (for dental consultation).

Night Life/Entertainment

San Diego has a lot to offer in the area of entertainment and night life. One should definitely make advance reservations for some shows and performances, especially in the larger hotels.

Current information on entertainment can be found in the two daily newspapers: "San Diego Union" and "San Diego Tribune."

Other publications with information on entertainment are: "San Diego Reader," "North Country Entertainer," "Where" and "Today." These publications are usually available in larger stores or hotels free of charge. Information on entertainment by telephone is available by calling, Tel: (619) 239-9696.

Restaurants: Alfonso's, 12151 Prospect Avenue in La Jolla, Mexican restaurant, Tel: (619) 454-2232.

Anthony's Fish Grotto, 1360 Harbor Drive, good fish restaurant, Tel: (619) 232-5103.

Benihana of Tokyo, 477 Camino del Rio, Japanese steak house, Tel: (619) 298-4666.

Carino's Italian Restaurant and Pizza, 7508 La Jolla Boulevard.

Casa de Banini, 2660 Calhoun Street, Tel: (619) 297-8211.

Chart House, 2760 Shelter Island Drive, Tel: (619) 222-2216.

Old Spaghetti Factory, 275 Fifth Avenue, Tel: (619) 233-4323.

Hyatt Islandia, 1441 Quivira Road, (all you can eat), Tel: (619) 224-3541.

T. D. Hays, 4135 Ocean Boulevard, Tel: (619) 270-6850.

Shopping: Kobey's Swap Meet, 3500 Sports Arena Boulevard, established in 1980, has become the largest flea market in the region where just about everything can be purchased at very reasonable prices. Thursday to Sunday from 7 am to 3 pm, admission: $1, children under 12, free, Tel: (619) 226-0650.

Balboa Park — Spanish Village between the zoo and the Natural History Museum, Tel: (619) 233-9050.

Downtown — Gaslamp Quarter; Seaport Village; Horton Plaza; Farmers Bazaar, 205 Seventh Avenue, Tel: (619) 233-0281.

La Jolla — Coast Walk, 1298 Prospect Street, Tel: (619) 454-3031.
Mission Valley — Fashion Valley Center, 352 Fashion Valley Road, Tel: (619) 297-3381; Mission Valley Center, 1640 Camino del Rio North, Tel: (619) 296-6375.
Old Town — Bazaar del Mundo, 2754 Calhoun Street, Tel: (619) 296-3161; Old San Diego Square, 2479 Juan Street, Tel: (619) 298-9924; Squibob's Square, 2611 San Diego Avenue, Tel: (619) 296-1298.

Transportation

Airport: The San Diego International Airport, Lindbergh Field, 3165 Pacific Highway, Tel: (619) 231-5220 is located only 3 miles northwest of downtown San Diego. Inexpensive transportation between the airport and the downtown area is offered by the San Diego Transit Corporation buses (bus no. 2), Tel: (619) 233-3004.

By taxi, the trip to the airport costs $6 to $8.

Train Station: The train station is located at 105 Kettner Boulevard and Broadway in the centre of town. Amtrak not only offers good daily connections to Los Angeles, but also other interesting travel destinations. Tel: 1-800-648-3850 or 1-800-872-7245.

Bus Terminal: Also located in the downtown area of San Diego are the terminals for the two large bus lines: Continental Trailways, 310 West C and Union Street, Tel: (619) 232-2001; Greyhound, First Avenue and Broadway, Tel: (619) 239-9171.

Distances from San Diego to:
Tijuana 17 miles
Las Vegas 332 miles
Borrego Springs 91 miles
Phoenix 356 miles
Los Angeles 125 miles
San Francisco 507 miles
Palm Springs 141 miles
Salt Lake City 769 miles

Public Transportation: The San Diego Transit Corporation buses usually depart every 15 to 20 minutes and cost $1.

Information, timetables etc.: 100 16th Street, Tel: (619) 233-3004.

The fares for various taxi companies can vary quite substantially. An average is $2.40 for the first mile and $1.20 for each additional mile.

On the corner of Broadway and Fourth Street, one can purchase inexpensive daily tickets for the public transportation. A one day ticket costs $4, a two day ticket $6 and a three day ticket $8.

Important Addresses

Emergency (Police, Ambulance Fire): Tel: 911.

Coast Guard: Tel: (619) 295-3121.

Tourist Information: San Diego International Visitors Information Center, 11 Horton Plaza, First and F Street, Tel: (619) 236-1212.

San Diego Convention and Visitors Bureau, 1200 Third Avenue, Suite 824, Tel: (619) 232-3101.

Visitor Information Center, Old Town Plaza, 2645 San Diego Avenue, Tel: (619) 237-6770.

Visitor Information Center, 2688 East Mission Bay Drive, Tel: (619) 276-8200.

Information Center, House of Hospitality, Balboa Park, Tel: (619) 239-0512.

North Coast Visitors Center, 640 Via de Valle, Tel: (619) 481-1811.

Mexican Tourist Office, 600 B Street, Suite 1200, Tel: (619) 236-9314.

Weather Forecast: Tel: (619) 289-1212.

Travellers Aid: 1122 Fourth Avenue, Tel: (619) 232-7991; Travellers Aid (Airport), Tel: (619) 231-7361.

San Francisco

The banks of fog at Golden Gate hindered this bay from being discovered for quite a while. It was only in 1775 that a Spanish ship found this passage. Only one year later, the Spaniards built a military fortress on the northern point of the peninsula, and Junipero founded the Christian mission of San Francisco de Asis, which is named Mission Dolores today. Between these two points, the small settlement of El Paraje de Yerba Buena grew rapidly and was renamed San Francisco under American rule. The Spanish-Mexican settlers, called "Californios," divvied up the hills and valleys of San Francisco amongst themselves between 1776 and 1850. They also murdered, enslaved or drove out the Ohlons and Miwoks from the bay area. Since this took place with the blessing of the Catholic mission, the development of the still young city of San Francisco took almost a "normal" and "planned" course.

However, in 1848 James Marshall, the steward of an estate, discovered abundant gold on the slopes of the Sierras, only a day's trip from San Francisco. The settlement grew from a population of 600 to 40,000 in the course of only one year. Many of the newcomers lived in tents and wooden shacks, distrusting everyone and not placing much value on morals, justice and public order.

This major change in the course of events prompted the construction of the Central Pacific Railroad. When the Chinese coolies completed the trans-continental railroad from New York via Chicago to San Francisco on May 10, 1869, modern times returned to San Francisco with this pioneering achievement. The filthy streets and houses of the dilapidated shantytowns disappeared.

With the following years, San Francisco almost recovered to a state of normalcy. However, this proved to be the quiet before the storm: early in the morning of April 17, 1906, a powerful earthquake and the ensuing fires destroyed 80% of the city. The hands on the Ferry Building clock stopped at 5:07 am. The earthquake claimed over 700 lives and around a quarter of a million people (over half of the population of San Francisco) were homeless. In light of this, it is almost a miracle that the survivors could rebuild San Francisco in only five years. This renaissance is considered an extraordinary achievement in the turbulent history of this city even today.

San Francisco developed once more into one of the most beautiful cities in the world. Its praises were sung by millions as it became a preferred city — up until October 17, 1989. At exactly 5:07 pm, the clock on the Ferry Building stopped again when the Loma Prieta earthquake (named after a mountain located near the epicentre) shook the city once more. The earthquake claimed over 100 lives; houses, streets and bridges were destroyed. Ripped cables and phone lines crept out of crevices in the earth. Cable cars derailed and escaping gas caused devastating blazes. The earthquake hit the Victorian houses in the Marina district especially hard — one of the most beautiful districts in the city. In contrast, the skyscrapers in the downtown area remained virtually untouched. For the first time, the precautionary measures were put to the test — and successfully at that. The massive shock resistant constructions in the foundations of these skyscrapers could absorb most of the vibrations and the buildings themselves were built to sway up to two meters. The very next morning after the earthquake, the Pacific Stock Exchanged was open for business and the television stations competed for the highest ratings by offering dramatic film coverage, while a fantastic solidarity developed among the people.

San Francisco, on the tip of the 32 mile long peninsula at the "Golden Gate" still stands on the 40 hills. Even after this catastrophe it remains one of the most beautiful cities on the globe. The hilly landscape dictates the characteristic layout of the streets and defines, to a great extent, the unique beauty of this city. San Francisco also has a constantly changing history with a number of ups and downs. Its residents demonstrate an unbroken optimism. San Francisco is a place where a broad range of extreme positions and lifestyles are tolerated and accepted within a relatively small area. It might be exactly this unique coexistence of the most contrasting lifestyles which makes the city unparalleled.

San Francisco / Sights

Alcatraz Island: This famous penal island is in the San Francisco Bay and can be easily seen from Fisherman's Wharf. The Spanish named the island "Islas de los Alcatraces," the island of pelicans. From 1934 to 1963, the prison on this island of rock gained the reputation of being "escape proof." It was for this reason that the most dangerous criminals in the United States were imprisoned here. Al Capone and Machine Gun Kelly are two infamous examples. Today, this island is under the administration of the National Park Service, offering tours to visitors. The ferries are often completely booked during the peak season from May to September. For this reason reservations are recommended. Reservations can be made by contacting Ticketron, P.O. Box 26430, San Francisco, California 94126, Tel: (415) 546-2805. The Alcatraz ferry departs from Pier 41 and costs $5. Red & White Ticket Counter, Pier 41, Fisherman's Wharf, Tel: (415) 546-2896.

Cable Cars: These famous tourist attraction is the only moving national monument in the United States. Invented by the cable manufacturer Andrew Smith Hallidie in 1870, they still operate according to the same principle today.

The cars are pulled by a steel cable, which runs under the streets at a speed of about 10 to 13 miles per hour. The cars are pulled up the hills and then are turned on a turntable to run in the opposite direction. The first cable car route went in to operation on the east side of Nob Hill in 1873. Around 1890, the cable car system was comprised of a total of almost 120 miles with 600 cable cars. After expensive renovations, 44 cable cars have been in operation once more since 1984 on a total of 10 miles of tracks. The cable cars run daily from 6 am to 1 pm on three routes: from the corner of Powell and Market Street to Fisherman's Wharf, from the corner of Powell and Market Street to Victoria Park and the California Route from Market Street to Van Ness Avenue. Cable car fare is $2.

Cable Car Museum, Powerhouse and Car Barn: The central powering mechanism, interesting details presented in the museum and some of the first cable cars can be seen at the corner of Washington and Mason Street. Tel: (415) 474-1887.

Chinatown: This city within a city begins at the pagoda style gateway near Bush Street and ends on Columbus Avenue. The main street is Grand Avenue, dominated by tourists. In this exotic world, restaurants, tea houses, theatres, bars, nightclubs, souvenir shops, schools and temples are packed along the streets.

Especially interesting is the *Chinese Cultural Center,* 750 Kearny Street, on the third floor of the Holiday Inn Hotel.

Chinese Historical Society of America, 17 Adler Place at Grand Avenue, Tel: (415) 391-1188.

Temples which are open to the public are: Kong Chow Temple, Clay and Stockton Street, Tien Hou Temple, 125 Waverly Place and Buddha's Universal Church, 720 Washington Street.

Civic Center: Bordered by Market, Hayes and Franklin Streets and Golden Gate Avenue is a group of several impressive buildings around a central square. These include the 300 foot tall *City Hall,* with its huge dome, the neighbouring *Opera House,* the *Veterans Memorial Building* (this was the location of the signing of the Uno Charta on June 26, 1945), the *State Building,* the *Federal Building,* the *Main Public Library* and the *Civic Auditorium.* In the various buildings are museums and large halls for art and cultural exhibitions. Information is available by contacting Tel: (415) 552-8338.

Map of Western San Francisco

N · 0 — 1 km

PACIFIC OCEAN

Golden Gate Bridge

Golden Gate National Recreation Area

THE PRESIDIO

California St.

Park Presido Blvd.

Cliff House

Geary Blvd.

Balboa St.

Fulton St.

Conservatorium

GOLDEN GATE PARK

Planetarium

Stanyan St.

Lincoln Way

Judah St.

Moraga St.

7th Av.

Ortega St.

Sunset Blvd.

19th Av.

Quintara St.

Great Highway

Taraval St.

Mt. Davidson

San Francisco Zoo

Sloat Blvd.

SAN FRANCISCO

- San Francisco Bay
- Fisherman's Wharf
- Little Italy
- Lombard St.
- Divisadero St.
- Broadway
- South Van Ness Av.
- Washington St.
- California St.
- Oakland Bay Bridge
- Pine St.
- Geary Blvd.
- Market St.
- Turk St.
- Civic Center
- Howard St.
- Folsom St.
- Fulton St.
- Opera
- Oak St.
- Market St.
- Highway 101
- Fwy.
- Southern
- 3rd Street
- 16th St.
- Lick
- Embarcadero Fwy.
- Castro St.
- James
- Army St.
- to Los Angeles

Financial District: This is the location of most of the impressive skyscrapers in the city. These include the 850 foot tall *Transamerica Building* as well as the 650 foot high *Bank of America Building.* Definitely worth seeing is the *Embarcadero Center* located nearby with the impressive reception area of the Hyatt Regency Hotel.

Fisherman's Wharf: The harbor district at the end of Taylor Street and the beginning of the Embarcadero is one of the most colourful and popular tourist areas in the city. This region is one big stage with a continuing performance of characters, street musicians, artists, jugglers, magicians, break dancers and of course everything else one might expect to find in a tourist area like souvenir shops, restaurants, a wax museum and, believe it or not, the Believe It or Not Museum.

Golden Gate Promenade: Beginning at the Victorian and Aquatic Park at the end of Jefferson Street south of Fisherman's Wharf, the Golden Gate Promenade extends to Fort Point at the base of the Golden Gate Bridge almost 4 miles. It is a coastal promenade offering a great deal of variety. Depending on the season and one's personal interests, one can spend up to an entire day strolling along the promenade.

Directly at the beginning of the promenade is the *Fort Mason Center,* which is the site of a former military complex which has been transformed into a cultural centre with galleries, studios, a small theater and various shops. This area also hosts various special events. Information is available by contacting Tel: (415) 441-5705.

The promenade then leads by a yacht harbor on Marina Boulevard, lined with beautiful Victorian houses. Following this is the *Palace of Fine Arts,* a round building supported by massive columns built in classical architecture. It was built for the international Panama-Pacific Exhibition in 1915. Directly adjacent to this is the *Exploratorium,* well suited to those who enjoy experimenting with hands-on exhibitions. This museum for science, art and human perception has a total of 650 exhibits. The famous physical scientist Frank Oppenheimer founded the Exploratorium in 1969 and acted as director of the museum until his death in 1985. The Exploratorium is open Wednesdays from 10 am to 9:30 pm, Thursday to Sunday from 10 am to 5 pm and is closed Mondays and Tuesdays. Admission is $6 for adults, $4 for students, and $2 for visitors between the ages of 6 and 17. Admission is free of charge on every first Wednesday of each month and after 6 pm every Wednesday. Information: Tel: (415) 561-0360. The Exploratorium, 3601 Lyon Street, San Francisco, California 94123, Tel: (415) 563-7337.

Directly near the Exploratorium is the *Presidio of San Francisco*. This two and a half square mile complex is similar to a park and is now home to the 6th US Army Division. It was originally the location of the first fort built by the Spanish conquerors in 1776. Remaining of the old buildings is the Commandante's Headquarters, which now serves as an officers' club. The complex is open to the public, as is the *Presidio Army Museum*, corner of Lincoln Boulevard and Funston Avenue; open Tuesday to Sunday from 10 am to 4 pm, Tel: (415) 561-4115.

The Golden Gate Promenade finally ends at *Fort Point,* which has remained virtually unchanged from the time it was built from 1861-1865 before the Civil War. The walls of this fortress are 12 feet thick. Thirty minute tours begin every full hour. There is also an interesting film on the Golden Gate Bridge, shown daily 3:30 pm. The fort is open daily from 10 am to 5 pm, Tel: (415) 556-1693.

Golden Gate Bridge: This beautiful bridge, built in 1937, spans the "Golden Gate" connecting San Francisco with Marin County and Highway 101. Along with the cable cars and the Transamerica building, this bridge counts as one of the landmarks of San Francisco. It is one of the longest suspension bridges ever built with a total length of over 8,950 feet, and 4,195 feet separate the two main towers, which reach a height of about 750 feet above the bay, making them the highest in the world. The bridge itself is 220 feet above the water. When heading south, toll is charged; heading north, the use of the bridge is free of charge.

Golden Gate Park: Within this very beautiful park, there is a lake which is bordered by the botanical gardens, public sports facilities, and zoologically interesting areas with animals typical to the North American continent as well as very interesting museums.

Academy of Science: The Academy of Science is made up of a number of museums: North American Hall, Simpson African Hall, the Steinhart Aquarium and the Morrison Planetarium. It is one of the largest of its kind in the United States. General Information: Tel: (415) 752-8262; information on laser shows: Tel: (415) 221-0168. Admission is $4, with free admission on the first Wednesday of every month; admission to the planetarium costs an additional $3.

This museum complex is located on Middle Drive in Golden Gate Park and is open daily from 10 am to 5 pm.

Asian Art Museum: In 1959, Avery Brundage, the former president of the Olympic Committee, donated his extensive collection of Asian art to the city of San Francisco. In 1966, the Asian Art Museum was opened directly next to the Japanese gardens.

The museum is open daily from 10 am to 5 pm. Admission is $4 with free admission on the first Wednesday of each month. Information: Tel: (415) 751-2500.

De Young Memorial Museum: Art from ancient Egypt as well as classical Greek and Roman art make up the focal point of this museum. Other attractions include works by the European masters like Rembrandt, El Greco, Goya, Hals, Monet, Tiepolo and Watteau.

The museum is open from Wednesday to Sunday from 10 am to 5 pm. Admission is $3 with free admission on the first Wednesday of each month. Tel: (415) 750-3659.

Lombard Street: This street is known, especially through films and television, as the "crookedest street in the world." It is only as long as a city block and has ten hairpin curves and a grade of 40% leading from Hyde Street to Leavenworth Street.

North Beach: North Beach is the Italian quarter of San Francisco, in which the streets are full of activity and life, especially in the area around Broadway and Columbus Avenue where the bars and nightclubs are located. In addition, a stroll through the various art galleries, bookshops, and a visit to the restaurants and artists' pubs is also worthwhile. *Coit Memorial Tower* offers a beautiful view of the city including the Golden Gate Bridge. This tower is located at the top of the 300 foot high *Telegraph Hill*.

San Francisco / Practical Information
Accommodation
Camping: Candlestick RV Park, 120 RV sites, $30, shuttle service to the downtown area, 650 Gilman Street, reservations are recommended

---

San Francisco Bay is the golden gate to the shimmering and quaking city of San Francisco ▶

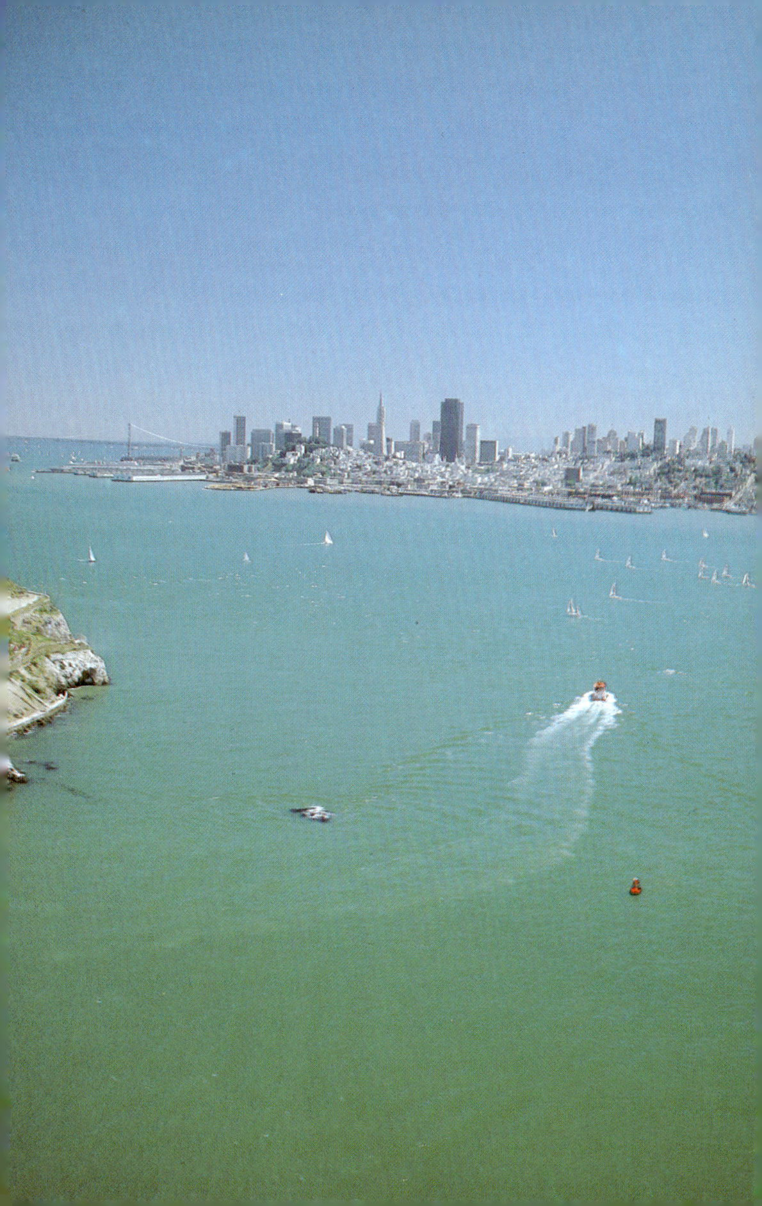

during the summer months, Tel: (415) 822-2299 or 1-800-888-CAMP.

San Francisco RV Park, 200 RV sites, $28 to $36 for two persons, additional person $2 to $3, 250 King Street between 3rd and 4th Street at the end of Interstate 280, Tel: (415) 986-8730.

Pacific Park RV Park, 257 RV sites priced from $28 to $30, 700 Palmetto in Pacifica south of San Francisco, Tel: (415) 355-2112 or 1-800-992-0554 within California, and 1-800-822-1250 within the United States.

San Francisco North/Petaluma KOA, 312 tent and RV sites priced from $22 to $28 for two persons, additional person $2 to $4, approximately 37 1/2 miles north of San Francisco, 20 Rainsville Road in Petaluma, reservations are recommended, Tel: 1-800-992-CAMP and (707) 763-1492.

Youth Hostels/YMCA/Guest Houses: San Francisco International Hostel, Building 240, Fort Mason, maximum length of stay 3 days, arrival time between 7 and 10 am, convenient location near many of the attractions, reservations are recommended, $8 for members, Tel: (415) 771-7277.

Youth Hostel Central, 116 Turk Street, between the Civic Center and Union Square, reservations are recommended, $8 for members, Tel: (415) 346-7835.

European Guest House, 761 Minna Street, $15 per person, reservations are recommended, Tel: (415) 861-6634.

Globe Hostel, 10 Hallum Place, $30 for one and two persons, additional person $15 in dormitories, reservations are recommended, Tel: (415) 431-0540.

Motels/Hotels: All Seasons, $40 to $75 for one and two persons, additional person $6, 417 Stockton Street, Tel: (415) 986-8737.

Amsterdam, $45 to $70 for one and two persons, additional persons $6, 749 Taylor Street, Tel: (415) 673-3277.

Atherton Hotel, 685 Ellis Street, good hotel at the beginning of a less pleasant area of town, $50 to $70 for two persons, reservations are recommended, Tel: (415) 474-5720.

Bel Air, $45 to $70 for one and two persons, additional person $8, 344 Jones Street, Tel: (415) 771-3460.

Essex Hotel, priced from $45 for one and two persons, additional person $6, about 20% less expensive during the winter, 648 Ellis Street Tel: (415) 474-4664 or 1-800-45ESSEX.

Marina Hotel, priced from $35 for one and two persons, additional person $5, 2576 Lombard Street, Tel: (415) 776-7500.

Banks: All of the leading banks can be found in the financial district.

Beaches and Swimming: Ocean Beach at the end of Golden Gate Park, China Beach and Baker Beach on the South Bay and a small beach at Aquatic Park near Fisherman's Wharf are the most well known beaches in San Francisco. In addition, there are eight indoor swimming pools, operated by the San Francisco Recreation and Park Department. Information: Tel: (415) 558-3643.

Car Rental: All of the larger rental agencies have offices in the San Francisco International Airport and in the centre of the city. However, at most of these, one must reserve a vehicle in advance. A more inexpensive alternative to these is the local agency Bay Area Rent-A-Car, 111 Stevenson Street near Market Street. The customer must be at least 25 years of age and must present a credit card. Price: $20 to $25 per day with unlimited mileage, Tel: (415) 362-7564. Other inexpensive agencies are: Bob Leach's Autorental San Francisco, 435 South Airport Boulevard, South San Francisco, Tel: (415) 583-2727; Rent a Wreck, 555 Ellis Street, Tel: (415) 776-8700.

Medical Care/Hospitals: First aid and medical attention is available at Access Health Care/Firstcare Corporation, 1604 Union Street near Franklin Street, Tel: (415) 775-7766.

Children's Hospital of San Francisco, 3700 California Street (Laurel Heights), Tel: (415) 387-8700, 24 hour service.

City Chiropractic Center, 37 Grove Street at the Civic Center, Tel: (415) 552-2999 or (415) 621-0961; on duty Mondays, Wednesdays and Fridays from 8:30 am to 6:15; Tuesdays, Thursdays and Saturdays from 9 am to 12:30 pm, closed Sundays.

Medical Offices Health Service, 786 Haight Street (Western Addition), Tel: (415) 467-0985 or (415) 467-4890, on duty Mondays to Fridays from 8:30 am to 6 pm.

Saint Francis Memorial Hospital, 900 Hyde Street on Union Square, Tel: (415) 775-4321.

Saint Mary's Hospital and Medical Center, 450 Stayon Street, (Haight Ashbury), Tel: (415) 668-1000.

University of California, Parnassus Avenue at Third Avenue, Tel: (415) 476-1000 or 1-800-792-0772; on call 24 hours.

Dental Care: San Francisco Dental Office, 132 The Embarcadero, Tel: (415) 777-5115.

Night Life and Entertainment: San Francisco has a lot to offer in the way of entertainment and night life. In the North Beach area and between the Embarcadero and Fisherman's Wharf, there is a wide selection of pubs, bars and other locales. The opera, the ballet and symphony orchestra in San Francisco enjoy world renowned. These can all be found in the Civic Center located on Van Ness Avenue at Grove Street, Tel: (415) 864-3330 (opera) or Tel: (415) 762-BASS (ballet); Davies Symphony Hall, Van Ness Avenue and Grove Street, Tel: (415) 431-5400. In addition to these, a number of smaller theatre companies flourish in this city, offering excellent theatre performances.

A historical and mobile landmark — the cable cars of San Francisco

Restaurants: In the shopping areas listed below are also a number of good restaurants and cafés in lower to upper price categories. In the higher price categories, one should definitely make reservations. Shorts and T-shirts are inappropriate in these restaurants. A few selected addresses:
La Buena Vista, 2765 Hyde Street, directly opposite of the cable car terminal at Fisherman's Wharf.
The Iron Horse, 19 Maiden Lane, Tel: (415) 362-8133, north Italian cuisine.
New Joe's, 347 Glory Street, Tel: (415) 989-6733, traditional Italian cuisine.
Alioto's, Tel: (415) 673-0183, directly on Fisherman's Wharf, serving Italian cuisine and all types of meat dishes with a picturesque view of the bay, upper price category.
Chic's Place, Pier 39, serving seafood specialities, middle price category.
Harris', 2100 Van Ness Avenue, Tel: (415) 673-1888, specialising in steaks, upper price category.
Chinatown: Golden Dragon, 816 Washington Street, Tel: (415) 398-3920, inexpensive.
King Tin, 826 Washington Street, next door to the Golden Dragon, Tel: (415) 982-8228, inexpensive with a very authentic atmosphere.
Empress of China, 838 Grant Avenue, 6th Floor, Tel: (415) 434-1345, middle price category.
Kan's, 708 Grant Avenue, Tel: (415) 982-2388, middle price category.
Imperial Palace, 919 Grant Avenue, Tel: (415) 982-4440, upper price category.
Liao's Restaurant, 835 Hyde Street, Tel: (415) 776-7538, about four blocks south of Chinatown, large portions and inexpensive.
Japantown: Benihana of Tokyo, 1737 Post Street, Tel: (415) 563-4844, middle price category.
Shopping: San Francisco's shopping centres count among the city's attractions. In addition to the Fisherman's Wharf Zone, these include the nearby shopping centres "The Cannery," a former fruit canning factory, and Ghirardelli Square, which was a chocolate factory up until the 1960's when the influx of tourists held the promise of larger profits. Today, Ghirardelli Square is home to almost 80 stores and restaurants. Other shopping areas are Pier 39 at the beginning of Stockton Street, the Embarcadero Center bordered by Sacramento, Battery, Clay and Drumm Streets, and of course Chinatown and Japantown.

A wide selection of exclusive shops and boutiques can be found in the Union Square area.

There is a Safeway supermarket on Marina Boulevard near the fort Mason Center, where one can buy groceries and supplies for a camping tour at inexpensive prices. Good, inexpensive camping equipment can be found in the California Surplus Sales at 1107 Mission Street.

The "Sutter 500 International Book Store" at 500 Sutter Street (Downtown) has a broad selection of books and periodicals and also stocks books and magazines in foreign languages. It is open from 8:30 am to 10 pm, closed Sundays. Other stores and newsstands with international publications are: European Book Co. 925 Larkin Street, Tel: (415) 474-0626. Harold's News, corner of post and Taylor Streets, Tel: (415) 474-2937.

Sports: In Candlestick Park, 8 miles south of San Francisco on Highway 101, one can watch the Giants baseball team and the 49ers football team in action. Information: Tel: (415) 468-2249.

The Golden Gate Park is a paradise for the active traveller. It is the perfect place to jog, cycle, for a ride on horseback, to play golf or tennis or paddle in a boat over the lake.

Bicycle Rental: Spokes and Things, 150 College Avenue, corner of 9th and Fulton Street near the main entrance to the Golden Gate Park. This agency rents out bicycles and tandems by the hour, half day and full day. It is open daily from 10 am to 5 pm. Other bicycle rentals near Golden Gate Park are concentrated along Stanyan Street.

A popular spot for boating and fishing is Lake Merced. Near this lake are also various golf courses and tennis courts. Information is available from the San Francisco Recreation and Park Department, Tel: (415) 558-3643.
→*Beaches and Swimming, this entry.*

Transportation: The public transportation system in San Francisco is very good and inexpensive. The San Francisco Municipal Railway, MUNI for short, includes buses, streetcars and the famous cable cars. A ticket for each of these costs 85 cents including transfers. Information is available under Tel: (415) 673-6864.

The subway system connects San Francisco with the cities to the east of the bay. Within San Francisco is the Bay Area Rapid Transit, BART for short, running from Market Street to the San Francisco Zoo and out to the southern regions of the city. Tickets cost 80 cents to one dollar.

Information: Tel: (415) 788-BART. The San Trans buses operate to Palo Alto in San Mateo County which lies to the south of San Francisco. Information: Transbay Terminal, First and Mission Street, Tel: (415) 761-7000. Continental Trailways, Transbay Terminal, Tel: (415) 982-6400.

Greyhound, Greyhound Depot, 50 7th Street near Market Street, Tel: (415) 433-1500.

Green Tortoise, First and Natoma Streets behind the Transbay Terminal, Tel: (415) 821-0803.

Taxis: Fares for taxis start at around $1.30 for the first mile and 50 cents to $1.20 for each additional mile.

Trains: the Amtrak station is located on 16th Street and Wood Avenue in Oakland. This is the terminal station for all of the train routes to San Francisco. Shuttle service is offered to the Transbay Terminal. Information: Tel: (415) 983-8512.

Ship: Ferries depart from Piers 41, 43 and 1 (Ferry Building) for the attractions in the San Francisco area and to Sausalito, Larkspur, Tiburon and Angel Island. The prices range from $5 to $8.50. Information: Tel: (415) 332-6600 and (415) 546-2815.

Air Travel: The San Francisco International Airport is 15 miles south of the city near San Mateo directly on the bay. The Oakland International Airport on the eastern side of the bay offers quite often a good and less expensive alternative for domestic flights.

Important Addresses

Police, Fire, Emergency: Tel: 911.

Main Post Office: Seventh and Mission Street, additional post offices can be found on Fillmore Street between Union and Lombard Street. Post offices are open weekdays from 9 am to 5:30 pm and Saturdays from 9 am to 1 pm.

If one encounters problems, one should contact *Travellers Aid,* 38 Mason Street, San Francisco, Tel: (415) 781-6738.

Tourist Information Office: San Francisco Visitors Bureau, 1390 Market Street, San Francisco, California 94102, Tel: (415) 626-5500.

For tourists who have already arrived in San Francisco, the best address is the San Francisco Visitors Information Center in Hallidie Plaza, Powell and Market Street, open Mondays to Fridays from 9 am to 5:30 pm, Saturdays from 9 am to 3 pm, Sundays from 10 am to 2 pm, Tel: (415) 391-2000.

San Francisco Convention and Visitors Bureau, 201 Third Street, Suite 900, San Francisco, California 94103-3185, Tel: (415) 974-6900.

San Luis Obispo

San Luis Obispo is a small town of 35,000 and has a high proportion of artists. It is located around 200 miles from Los Angeles. Of interest here is the beautifully laid out *Mission Plaza*. The mission of San Luis Obispo de Tolosa was the fifth mission founded by Serra in 1772 for the Chumash Indians. The lifestyle of this tribe is very well presented in the *County Historical Museum* 696 Monterey Street.

Accommodation

Camping: El Chorro Regional Park Campground, 50 RV sites, $8 per site, 5 miles north on Highway 1, Tel: (805) 595-2359.

Motels: Best Western Sommerset Manor, from $45 for one and two persons, additional person $3, 1895 Monterey Street, Tel: (805) 544-0973. Villa San Luis Motel, from $40 for one and two persons, additional person $4, 1670 Monterey Street, Tel: (805) 534-8071.

San Simeon/Hearst Castle

If one leaves the Big Sur coastal region, the coastline gradually becomes flatter, losing a portion of its rugged beauty. For this reason, not too many tourists would go to San Simeon if it were not for the elaborate *Hearst Castle* on the opposite side of the coastal road. This building has since been declared a State Historical Monument. In 1919, William Randolph Hearst, one of the most influential men in the United States, began with the construction of this impressive palace, which had still not been completed when he died in 1951. The complex is so large that the two tours offered last two to four hours, leading through the different parts of the complex. Especially impressive is the dining hall, which is similar to a cathedral as well as the Neptune pool, embellished with mythological statues.

Tours are offered from June 1 to August 31 daily from 8 am to 4 pm and from September 1 to May 31 daily from 8:30 am to 3:30 pm. Tickets cost

---

Victorian houses are as much a part of San Francisco's profile as the towering skyscrapers ▶

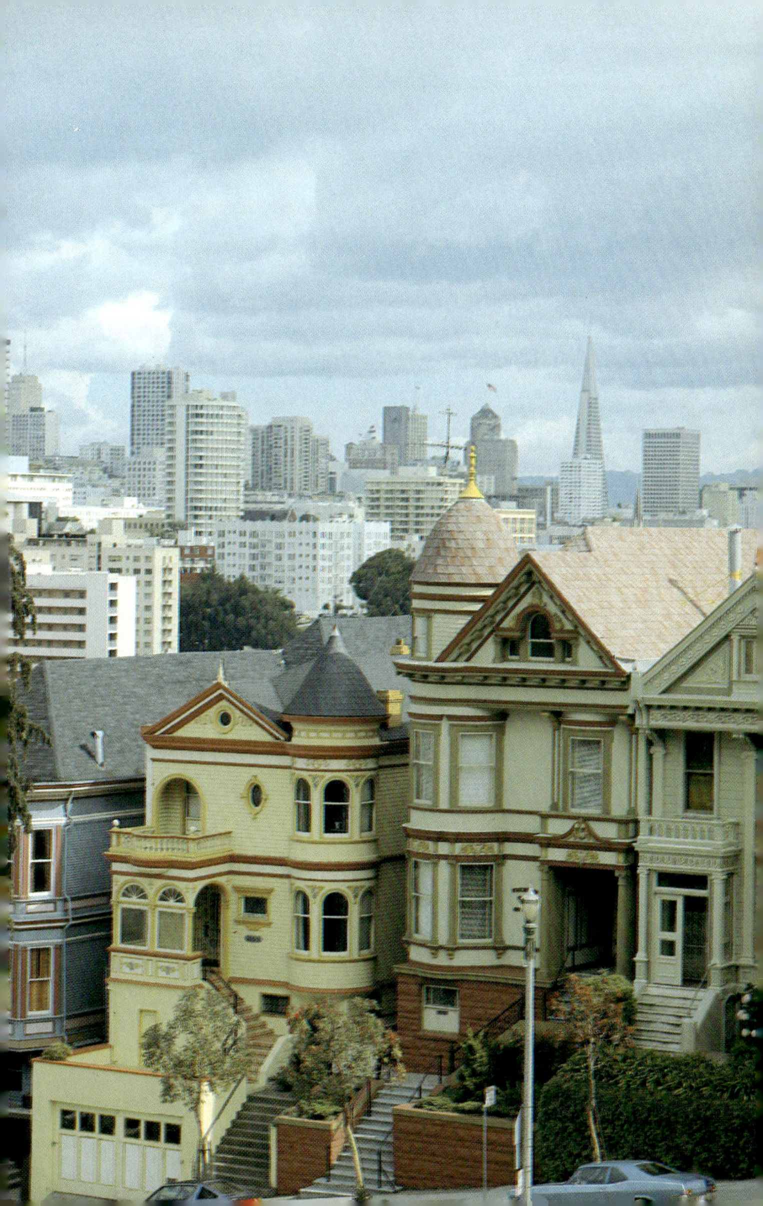

$12. For a first visit to the castle, Tour A is recommended. If one has not made reservations in advance, then it is a good idea to arrive at the visitor center when it opens. Reservations can be made up to 60 days in advance by contacting: Ticketron, P.O. Box 26430, San Francisco, California, 94126, Tel: (415) 393-6914 or (808) 927-4622.

San Simeon, Hearst Castle / Practical Information
Accommodation
Camping: San Simeon State Beach Campground, 115 tent and RV sites, $6 per site, 5 miles south on Highway 1, Tel: (805) 927-4509.
Motel: El Rey Inn, $50 to $60 for one and two persons, additional person $5, 9260 Castillo Drive, Tel: (805) 927-3998.
Restaurants: Europa Restaurant, 9240 Castillo Drive, middle price category, reservations are recommended, Tel: (805) 927-3087.

Santa Barbara

Santa Barbara is only 95 miles north of Los Angeles, situated directly on the Pacific coast and the beautiful slopes of the Santa Ynez mountains. This atmosphere of this city has a strong Spanish influence, with red tiled roofs and archways. Located in Santa Barbara on Los Olivos and Laguna Street is the queen of the 21 Californian missions. Serra built this only four years after the city was founded on December 4, 1786. The small chapel as well as the mission's church are doubtlessly the most beautiful of their kind in California. A visit to this mission is very informative and well worthwhile. Admission is $1; Tel: (805) 682-4149.

The *Botanical Garden* at 1212 Mission Canyon Road was also laid out by the Franciscans at the same time that they built the Indian Dam and an aqueduct.

On the way from the mission to the botanical garden is the *Museum of Natural History,* located at 2559 Puesta del Sol Road. The evolutionary history of both man and animals is presented here. Admission is free of charge, Tel: (805) 682-4711. The beautiful inner city of Santa Barbara is best explored on foot. One must go down State Street to the intersection of De La Guerra and then up to Victoria Street. There, one can turn right, down the street for one block to Anacapa Street to get back to the starting point. In this area are not only very beautiful, historically significant buildings, but also nice shops, cafés and restaurants. An especially impressive building is the *County Courthouse* at 1100 Anacapa Street, which is called the nations most beautiful public building by the residents of Santa Barbara. From the tower of this building, *El Mirador,* one has a wonderful panorama of the city. Admission is free of charge; Tel: (805) 966-1611.

The *Scenic Drive,* with its 15 points of interest will provide a good overall impression of the city.

The *Our Lady of Mount Carmel Church* is built in the mission style typical for California. It is located at 1300 East Valley Road, in an area with many beautiful mansions.

Santa Barbara / Practical Information

Accommodation

Camping: El Patio Camper Village, 110 RV sites, $18 to $24 for two persons, additional person $3, 4040 Calle Real, Tel: (805) 687-7614.

Motels: Best Western Encina Lodge, $75 to $90 for one and two persons, additional person $6, 2220 Bath Street, Tel: (805) 682-7277.

The Best Western chain has additional hotels in Santa Barbara.

Vagabond Inn, from $55 for one and two persons, additional person $6, 1920 State Street, Tel: (805) 569-1521.

Vagabond Inn, from $55 for one and two persons, additional person $6, 2819 State Street, Tel: (805) 687-6444.

Polynesian Motel, 433 West Montecito Street, from $50 for one and two persons, additional person $10, reservations are recommended, Tel: (805) 963-7851.

Sandpiper Lodge, 3525 State Street, $44 to $70 for one and two persons, additional person $7, reservations are recommended, Tel: (805) 687-5362.

Restaurants: The inner city centre offers a wide selection of restaurants. The coffee shops with small but tasty snacks and light meals are very popular.

The Cattlemen's Restaurant and Saloon, 3714 State Street in the Hotel "Sandmann Inn," sometimes with live entertainment, reservations are recommended, Tel: (805) 687-2468.

The Philadelphia House, 4422 Hollister Avenue, reservations are recommended, Tel: (805) 964-9924.

Shopping: There are a number of shops in the areas described and in the northwestern portion of the city is a large supermarket. A good bakery can be found at 831 Santa Barbara Street.

Transportation: The Santa Barbara Trolley Company has good connections to various points of interest. The terminal is Stearn's Wharf. Information: Tel: (805) 962-0209; price: $2.

Important Addresses

Santa Barbara Conference and Visitors Bureau, P.O. Box 299, Santa Barbara, California 93102, Tel: (805) 965-3021.

Visitors Bureau, 1330 State Street, open Mondays to Saturdays.

The most impressive of the Californian missions is found in Santa Barbara

Sequoia and Kings Canyon National Park

Two of the three species of sequoia trees found in the world are indigenous to the United States (→Redwood National Park). In some areas along the Pacific coastline, it is the sequoia semper virens, the gigantic evergreen trees, which are also called coastal redwoods due to their geographical location; growing on the western slopes of the Sierra Nevadas is the especially large species, the sequoiadendron giganteum. These trees, which survived the most recent ice age unlike many of the other species, can be found in Sequoia National Park at an altitude of 5,000 to 7,850 feet above sea level. Some of these trees are estimated to be over 1,000 years older than their relatives in the coastal areas. Due to their dimensions, they are known as "the greatest living things." The eastern regions of both of these parks are bordered by the Sierra Nevada mountain range, which includes the second highest mountain in the United States, Mount Whitney with an altitude of 14,447 feet. This mountain range is around 200 million years old and includes rugged canyons, rumbling waterfalls, numerous lakes and idyllic mountain meadows. The United States Congress gave these two areas the status of national parks in 1978.

Sequoia and Kings Canyon National Park / Sights

Two areas in each of these national parks stand apart as favoured destinations: Grant and Cedar Grove in Kings Canyon and Giant Forest as well as Mineral King in Sequoia National Park.

Grant Grove Region: The main attraction in this region is the 268 foot high sequoiadendron giganteum with a circumference of 105 feet: *General Grant Tree.* The uniformity of this tree resulted in its epithet, "the Christmas tree of the nation." Every year, a Christmas party is celebrated at its base. Northwest of the Big Stump entrance to the park, a number of tree stumps stand in Big Stump basin as a sad reminder of the wood processing industry of the past century. One huge tree was cut down in 1876 so that the world exposition in Philadelphia in 1876 could have a special attraction. Today, the *Centennial Stump* in the Grant Grove Region gives an impression of the former dimensions of this tree. Various hiking paths lead through this region. One of the most impressive in terms of the landscapes through which it leads it the hiking path to the *Park Ridge Firetower* in the southeast portion of the Grant Grove Region. Horses can also be rented.

Cedar Grove Region: After a 30 mile trip along the winding park road, one will arrive in this northern area of Kings Canyon National Park. The trip alone is fascinating, leading along the rugged Kings Canyon. The sunlight during the late afternoon makes the *Kings River,* tumbling over numerous cascades, especially beautiful. Before reaching the parking area at the end of the road, the *Roaring River Falls* offer the opportunity for a short detour: a walk along the path to *Zumwaldt Meadow* will prove interesting because of the informative signs along the way. Leading off from the parking area are a number of longer hiking trails. which are especially well suited for hikes through the mountains lasting several days. More easily accessible from here are the *Mist Waterfalls.* Backcountry permits, necessary for camping in the remote areas of the park, are available at the ranger station in Cedar Grove. Nearby is also a pack station where horses can be rented. Rental bicycles are also available.

Giant Forest Region: In this, probably the most attractive region in Sequoia National Park, the visitor will find some of the most beautiful groves of *giant sequoias.* With a height of 367 feet, Redwood National Park lays claim to the tallest tree in the world, but the Sequoia National Park claims to be home to the tree with the greatest overall dimensions: the *General Sherman Tree* reaches a height of 275 feet, has a diameter of 36 feet and a circumference of almost 105 feet. It is estimated to be 2,500 years old. The branches begin at a height of 130 feet above the ground, and even at this height, they measure over 6 feet in diameter. At the base of this giant is the one-mile *Congress Trail* leading by other impressive sequoias like the *Senate Group.* Somewhat further north, a trail branches off to Wolverton. This marks the beginning of a very beautiful mountain trail to the summit of the 11,164 foot *Alta Peak.* The hike there and back is around 14 miles. Those who consider this too much effort should rent a horse at the beginning of the trail. From Wolverton, there is also an easy trail leading to the mountain lakes *Heather* and *Pear* after around 5 miles. Also a very pleasant hike is around the *Round Meadow,* northeast of the Giant Forest Village as well as the 2 mile hike or car trip to the 6,700 foot *Moro Rock.* The summit offers a panorama of the Sierra Nevadas and the San Joaquin Valley. If one continues along the road past

Sequoia and Kings Canyon National Park

Moro Rock to Crescent Meadow, then one can take the mile-long trail to *Tharp's Log.* This is a small abode which was built in a tree stump. At the southern end of the Giant Forest Region, a nine-mile road leads off to *Crystal Cave.* From June 20 to the beginning of September, the visitor can take part in a tour, costing $1.50. These take place every half hour from 10 am to 3 pm, except for the break from noon to 1 pm.

Mineral King Region: This region is high in the southwestern portion of Sequoia National Park and is known to insiders as the most beautiful area in the Sierra Nevada mountain range. Near Hammond, a 25 mile, only partially paved road branches off of the US 198 to the east. This leads through an idyllic valley with beautiful lakes and numerous trails which are excellent for hikes through the mountains.

Sequoia and Kings Canyon National Park /
Practical Information

Accommodation

Camping: There are various, although rather simple, campsites scattered around the park. The price per night is about $4 to $6. Information is available in the visitor center.

Motels/Cottages: Both national parks have both motels and cottages.

Cedar Grove Lodge, from $65 for one and two persons, additional person $5, Tel: (209) 565-3617.

Stony Creek Lodge, from $60 for one and two persons, additional person $5, Tel: (209) 565-3650.

Giant Forest Lodge, $30 to $80 for one and two persons, additional person $6, Tel: (209) 565-3381.

Grant Grove Lodge, $30 to $55 for one and two persons, additional person $6, Tel: (209) 335-2314.

Information is available at the Visitor Center.

Medical Care: Within the park are the visitors centers and hotels can be found in Fresno, State Highway 180, 57 miles from Grand Grove and in Exeter, State Highway 198, 47 miles from Giant Forest.

Restaurants: In the main tourist areas within the park are a number of restaurants. At the nicer restaurants one should make reservations in the evenings.

Shopping: Grocery stores can be found in Cedar Grove Village, Stony Creek and Wilsonia. Camping equipment can be purchased in Cedar Grove Village, Giant Forest Village and Grant Grove Village; there are service stations in Cedar Grove Village, Lodgepole and Grant Grove Village.

Sports

Hiking: This park is ideal for hiking *(→Sights, this entry)*. Those who would like to camp in the hinterland will require a backcountry permit which is available in the Visitor Center free of charge. The rangers will be able to provide information on the entire area.

Horseback Riding: There are various riding stalls within the park, offering different tours on horseback. These last from one hour up to several days.

Wolverton Corrals and Pack Station, Tel: (209) 565-3445.

Mineral King Pack Station, Tel: (209) 561-3404.

Cedar Grove Pack Station, Tel: (209) 565-3464.

Important Addresses and Telephone Numbers

Police, Medical Attention: Tel: 911.

National Park Address: Superintendent, Sequoia and Kings Canyon National Park, Three Rivers, California 93271; Tel: (209) 565-3341.

Visitor Center/Information:

Lodgepole Visitor Center, Tel: (209) 565-3341.

Giant Forest Village Information Booth, Mineral King Ranger Station, Tel: (209) 565-3341.

Grant Grove Visitor Center, Tel: (209) 335-2315.

Cedar Grove Ranger Station, Tel: (209) 565-3341.

Seventeen Mile Drive

Seventeen Mile Drive is a car tour between Pacific Grove and Carmel. The $5 admission charge is by no means a wasted investment since the road through this landscape has a lot to offer. This picturesque coastline is home to sea lions, otters and seals as well as 17 exclusive golf courses which host the annual Bing Crosby Golf Tournament. In addition, there are a number of impressive mansions and the Monterey cypresses. This species of tree originates from the Pliocene Epoch and grows only on this five mile long section of coastline.

At each of the three entrances — Pacific Grove Gate, Carmel Gate and Highway 1 Gate — the visitor will be given an illustrated brochure which describes the points of interest along the way. Information is available by contacting Tel: (408) 372-5813 or (408) 624-9585.

Shopping

The shopping in California is diverse and can also be quite expensive, depending on where one shops. Just about everything imaginable is available. Of course, the typical souvenirs can be found at the individual attractions or larger cities.

Most supermarkets are open 24 hours, seven days a week.

Wine connoisseurs will be delighted to find a large selection of Califor-

Seventeen Mile Drive — a route between Carmel and Pacific Grove leading through picturesque landscapes along the coast

nian wines, which meanwhile rank among the best in the world. The selection of Californian wines in supermarkets is large, but imported wines are also available. The imported wines are often less expensive than the domestic.

Sights

The State of California can be subdivided into a number of regions, each interesting because of the different natural beauty, regional history, and attractions offered:

The Mother Load Country: This is the mane of the region which is home to a number of prospecting towns. Most of these are now abandoned ghost towns. The Mexican miners called the Mother Load "La Veta Madre" — a vein of gold which laced the western slope of the Sierra Nevadas. Mother Load Country begins north of Interstate 80 near Sierra City and ends southwest of Yosemite National Park near Mariposa. Those who would like to travel through the remnants of the gold rush era and experience a trace of these turbulent times, should take State Road 49 running north and south through the Mother Load Country.

The Wine Country: Indeed, there are a number of wine producing regions in California like San Joaquin Valley, Santa Cruz Mountain, Salinas Valley and Riverside County, but the Mecca for American wine connoisseurs and wine-drinking tourists is Napa Valley, often referred to as the Disneyland of wine.

The Redwood Country: This magnificent landscape with its impressive mammoth trees extends from Big Sur along the Pacific Coast up into the southwestern regions of Oregon *(→Redwood National Park)*.

The Desert Country: Even this arid and almost completely barren region of desert and cactus in the southeastern region of California has an attraction all its own. Especially from November to May, Palm Springs, Anza Borrego Desert State Park and Death Valley National Monument as well as Joshua Tree National Monument *(→individual entries)* are popular destinations.

The Big Sur Country: This beautiful, rugged strip of coastline at the point where the Santa Lucia Mountains ascend directly from the Pacific, is considered a haven for artists and individualists. Even in summer, when

Highway 1 in this region is often overcrowded, visitors will still be able to find a quiet spot with redwood groves in one of the side canyons. The coastal road is often veiled in fog during the morning hours, making it better to take a sightseeing drive in the afternoon.

Additional sights are, of course, the cities of San Francisco, Los Angeles and San Diego, each offering a unique metropolitan profile.

Solvang

In Solvang, only 45 miles west of Santa Barbara in Santa Ynez Valley, the visitor might think he has landed in Denmark. This city of 300 is considered the Danish capital of the United States. In 1911, a group of Danish educators set off in search of an appropriate location for a school for the traditions and culture of their homeland. They founded Solvang, which today is still considered exemplary for Danish architecture and culture. Neither the windmills nor the traditional gas lamps and horse-drawn streetcars are missing from the overall picture. Today, this Danish stronghold in California has become a tourist attraction, which is reflected by the number of shops at the center of this town.

During the course of a year, there are two main reasons for a visit to Solvang: Danish Days during the third weekend in September and the Solvang Theater Festival held in the amphitheatre from June to the end of September.

The *Old Mission Santa Ynez* at 1760 Mission Drive is a mission built in the typical Californian style, providing an interesting architectural contrast to the rest of Solvang. The mission houses a museum covering the history of this building, beginning with its establishment in 1804.

Speed Limits

Outside of city limits, the speed limit is 55 miles per hour (88 kilometres per hour). When driving through less populated areas, 65 mph is allowed (104 kmph). Within city limits, speed limits are from 25 to 30 mph (40 to 48 kmph) or as posted. One should definitely adhere to these regulations because speeding violations can be quite costly.

Sports and Recreation

In California as well as the rest of the United States, sports and recreational activities play a very important role. Football, baseball and basketball are the most popular spectator sports and mobilise masses. Recreational sports are also extremely popular.

Information on sporting events and public sports facilities is available at visitor information bureaus or in the sports section of the local newspapers. Recreational activities are diverse in California and, of course, aquatic sports are emphasised. Surfing, wind surfing, sailing and water-skiing count among these. Not only the Pacific coast plays an important role, but the lakes and rivers in the state's interior as well. The most popular area for aquatic sports is, however, along the Pacific coastline between San Francisco and San Diego in Southern California.

Golf and tennis are also extremely popular in California. Tourists will find ample and inexpensive facilities. Sports facilities are even abundant in the desert regions like Death Valley. The famous and meticulously manicured golf courses can be found on the Monterey Peninsula and in Palm Springs.

California is also popular for its ski areas. In some of these the lifts operate during the entire year. The most well known areas are in and around Lake Tahoe. Others can be found in Lassen Volcanic National Park, at Mammoth Lakes northeast of Fresno, in the San Bernardino mountains east of Los Angeles and at Clear Lake in the northern coastal regions of California.

Hiking enthusiasts will be especially pleased with the national parks in California. Even longer hiking tours are possible, like for instance over the John Muir Trail from Yosemite National Park to Mount Whitney in Sequoia National Park or the not yet completed Pacific Crest Trail which will lead through the entire state of California upon its completion. For most of these hiking tours, a special permit is required, which can be obtained without any problems at the park ranger stations. Detailed information is available by contacting the following addresses: Eastern Sierra Packers Association, 690 Main Street, Bishop, California 93514 or High Sierra Packers Association, Western Unit, P.O. Box 1362, Clovis, California 93613.

Telephones

When placing a long-distance call, one must first dial 1, the area code and the number. If the call is within the same area code, one must dial only the 1 followed by the number. When placing an international call, one must first dial 011 followed by the country code, the city code and the number, leaving off the initial 0 before the city code. Expect to pay around $7 for the first three minutes of an international/overseas call. The first three minutes are charged whether or not they are fully used. The country code for the United Kingdom is 44; for Ireland, 353.

Theatre →*Entertainment and individual entries*

Theft

In general, one will not encounter a high level of theft in California, but in large cities and anywhere where it is crowded, one does run the risk of having one's wallet or bag stolen. There are a number of pick-pockets at the tourist attractions as well.

Preventive Measures:
1. Only carry a small amount of cash or traveller's cheques.
2. It is helpful to have a money pouch or money belt to carry important documents. It is also good to carry money in the front and not the back pocket of trousers.
3. One should write down the numbers of traveller's cheques and credit cards and carry this separately. This will help in expediting the process should something be lost or stolen. In these cases one should contact a bank, savings and loan, or service centres of the credit card companies.
4. One should never leave valuables in the car.

If, despite these measures, something is stolen, contact the local police.

Time of Day

California has Pacific Time which is one hour earlier than Mountain Time (Denver), two hours earlier than Central Time (Chicago) and three hours earlier than Eastern Time (New York). In California it is eight hours earlier than in London (Greenwich Time).

Tourist Information

General information on California and all of the United States is available free of charge from:

United States Travel and Tourism Administration (USTTA)
14th Street and Constitution Avenue, NW
Washington DC, 20230
Tel: (202) 377-4003.

For information specifically on California contact:
California Office of Tourism
1121 L Street, Suite 103
Sacramento, California 95814
Tel: (916) 322-1396
or
California Office of Tourism
P.O. Box 9278, T98, Department 1003
Van Nuys, California 91409
Tel: 1-800-862-2543.

Most cities and national parks will have an official tourist information office or visitors center in which useful information on accommodation, special events, tours and hiking routes as well as regional and city maps and schedules for public transportation. Informational brochures on special attractions are also available there. These offices are always a good starting point when visiting a certain area.

National Park Information:
National Park Service
Fort Mason, Building 201
Bay and Franklin Streets
San Francisco, California 94123
Tel: (415) 556-0560.

National Forest Information:
U.S. Forest Service
Pacific Southwest Region
630 Sansome Street, Room 527
San Francisco, California 94111
Tel: (415) 750-2874.

State Park Information:
California State Park System
Department of Parks and Recreation
P.O. Box 942896
Sacramento, California 94296
Tel: (916) 445-6477.
Additional addresses can be found under individual entries,

Tourist Season

One will find that every season in California has its advantages and disadvantages. The high temperatures of the summer months tend to scare off most tourists from visiting the desert regions. Others choose just this time to travel to these regions because of the discounted hotel and motel prices. The cactus plants have bloomed by Indian summer, from the beginning of September to the middle of November. It is exactly this season, which is preferred for travel to this region. The temperatures in the south and southeast regions of California are still mild and the air on the coast is clear and dry.

From late autumn to spring, California's main attraction are the winter sport areas, while on the coast, the main attraction is observing the annual migration of the whales — a unique show of nature.

The natural profile of California is most diverse during the months before summer when much of the vegetation is in full bloom and when the rivers and lakes reach peak capacity. This is an especially impressive time to visit →*Yosemite National Park* since one of the main attractions in Yosemite Valley are the waterfalls, which have all but dried up by mid summer. Tourist season along the coast peaks during the summer months, making for higher expense for accommodation.

As a general rule: if one has not made plans to visit any particular attraction which is dependent on the season, then there is plenty to see and do in California the entire year over.

Travel Documents

For foreign visitors to the United States from the European Community, a visa is no longer necessary if staying only up to 90 days.

For visits lasting longer, one will need a visa which can be obtained from the US Embassies or General Consulates in one's home country. They will also be able to answer specific questions in regard to other entry requirements in individual cases.

Driving licences from foreign countries are valid in the United States; however, an international driving licence can help in a number of cases, like when renting a vehicle or if one should be stopped by the police.
→*Travelling in California, Insurance*

Travel in California

California's development over the years has been heavily influenced by the automobile. The highway system is excellent. Because of the high priority given to the automobile, this has quite markedly influenced the culture of California *(→Culture)* most noticeable by the number of drive-thru services offered.

By Car or Recreational Vehicle

A trip through California by car or camping vehicle offers a high level of independence when compared to travelling by bus, train or airplane. The fact that the infrastructure of California is based on the automobile makes a good argument for choosing this form of travel.

Another option which is growing in popularity is to rent a recreational vehicle, which offers a high level of comfort, especially when traversing the hot and arid southern regions of California.
→*Car Rental*

By Train

Travelling by train will offer a high level of comfort since the trains are usually equipped with a sleeping car, restaurant car and bar. However,

Travel in California

one cannot reach every destination by train although the Amtrak rail network encompasses 25,000 miles of tracks. For a trip in and around California, rail travel is less appropriate.

Amtrak (American Travel on Track) is the National Railway Passenger Corporation. Amtrak offers foreign visitors the US-Railpass valid for 45 days of unlimited travel for $299. In addition, there is also the inexpensive Regional US-Railpass, valid for travel in one of the four zones of the United States: west, central, south and north.

Information is available and reservations can be made by contacting the following number: Tel: 1-800-USA-RAIL.

By Bus

The routes of the two large bus lines, Greyhound and Continental Trailways, are so comprehensive in California that almost every destination can be reached easily by bus. Travel passes called the Ameripass are offered for 7 days ($189), 15 days ($249), and 30 days ($349). The prices for these are substantially less if purchased outside the United States. Information: Tel: 1-800-237-8211.

An interesting alternative, albeit with less destinations offered, is "Green Tortoise Alternative Travel." This service targets young people, offering more of the character of holiday travel. These buses offer service on the most popular routes in America and can be found in Alaska and Mexico as well as offering service between the cities of Boston, New York and San Francisco. The old but renovated buses sometimes have mattresses for weary travellers, making the capacity lower than one might expect. This however makes for a coherent group, planning various activities at the national parks along the way, etc.

Further Information:
Los Angeles, Tel: (213) 392-1990;
Santa Barbara, Tel: (805) 569-1884;
Santa Cruz, Tel: (408) 462-6437;
Outside California, Tel: 1-800-227-4766.

By Air

Of course the speediest way to get around is by airplane. A flight from the east coast to the west coast takes around $5^1/_2$ hours.

within California on the most travelled routes, there is a high level of competition making comparisons in price very worthwhile. The most inexpensive alternatives have been "Aircal" and "Western Airlines" in the past years. A shuttle plane is in operation between Los Angeles and San Francisco. On these, the traveller must forego any service, but the fares are noticeably lower. One will usually pay on board.

In addition, it is usually less expensive to depart from the smaller airports like Hollywood-Burbank, Oakland, Ontario or San Jose. The flight packs offered by a number of airlines are only worth the price if one plans to travel all over the United States. The various packages offered by American Airlines, Delta Airlines, Continental Airlines, Northwest Airlines and US-Air not only vary significantly in price, but also in limitations on travel routes, stop-overs and length of validity. Information on these is available at local travel agencies.

Hitchhiking

Hitchhiking is permitted within California, but the opinions regarding this differ greatly. The tendency for hitchhiking is definitely decreasing. Hitchhikers must be prepared for a long wait. The best option is at the truck stops near highways. Here one can ask the truck drivers for a ride. One should, however, not underestimate the dangers associated with hitchhiking, especially when travelling alone.

Travelling to California

Travelling to California by car offers the opportunity to make stops in the impressive western national parks and other points of interest along the way like Grand Canyon, Bryce and Zion Canyons, Lake Powell, Las Vegas and Salt Lake City. If time is scarce, this can be quite a strenuous drive, especially through the desert regions. Fuel is less expensive in towns than at the service stops along the highways. If making such an extensive trip by car, one should definitely consider joining an Automobile Club (→*Automobile Club*) which in addition to having maps, route plans and other information available, will pay off at the very latest if one's car breaks down in the middle of nowhere. In the western region of the United States, "nowhere" can take on huge dimensions.

Another option for travel to California is Amtrak, offering service from many of the major American cities. Information: 1-800-872-7245.

For information on bus travel to California, contact Greyhound/Trailways: 1-800-237-8211.

Most domestic and international flights will arrive at either the San Francisco International Airport (SFO) or the Los Angeles International Airport (LAX). Prices from London or Manchester to LA or San Francisco range from £311 to £520 depending on the season. The prices for domestic flights can vary greatly and change almost daily. Be aware of special youth rates and inexpensive stand-by fares.

Vegetation

California has been quite favoured by nature in terms of plant life. In many regions, the lush vegetation is astounding. Plant life alone is a large tourist attraction in California. Various types of cactuses can grow as high as a house. They transform barren desert regions (→*Joshua Tree National Monument, Death Valley National Monument*) into fascinating landscapes. Also impressive are the gigantic mammoth trees in the national parks (→*Redwood National Park, Sequoia and Kings Canyon National Park, Yosemite National Park*).

California's state flower is the poppy, which blooms here almost all year round. In April, several cities and towns celebrate "Golden Poppy Days."

Visas →*Travel Documents*
Weather →*Climate*

Yosemite National Park

Geologically, Yosemite National Park was formed 500 million years ago, when a shallow lake deposited thick sedimentary layers of eroded volcanic soil. Together with the folding of the mountains, magma from deep in the earth forced its way up, directly under the sedimentary stone. There, it cooled, forming granite which was then pushed to the surface. The glaciers from the past ice age eroded the uppermost layer of stone and transported it to the lower lying regions, while the granite monoliths were rounded to the dome formations typical for this national park. When the glaciers receded, the characteristic U-formed valleys remained.

In three locations in the park — Merced, Tuolumne and especially in the Mariposa Grove — one can see the almost 3,000 year old sequoias. These trees survived, unlike other related species, because of their location, protected from the glaciers.

Hundreds of years before the white man discovered Yosemite Valley, the Ahwahneechee Indians settled here to be followed later by the Miwok and the Paiute. The discovery of this valley is accredited to Walker in the year 1823. In the years and decades to follow, more and more people flooded into this area to marvel at the beauty of this region which was given the status of national park in 1890.

Yosemite National Park / Sights

The focal point of this nature reserve on the western slopes of the Sierra Nevadas, *Yosemite Valley,* lies amid the majestic mountains in the southwestern regions of the park. With the moisture from the Merced River and a number of smaller lakes, this valley is transformed into a blooming wonderland in the summer months, attracting two million visitors annually. The canyon walls tower over 300 feet against the backdrop of the mountains with an altitude of ten to thirteen thousand feet. This geological formation is the reason that many of the waterfalls drop over several levels before thundering to the depths of the valley. An especially impressive example of this are the *Yosemite Falls,* which fall a total of 2,425 feet over a number of cascades. The upper falls drop 1,430 feet; the cascades, another 670 and the lower falls, 325 feet. Especially popular with tourists are the *Bridalveil Waterfalls,* dropping 620 feet. One should not miss the *Vernal* (317 feet) and the *Nevada* (594 feet) waterfalls in the eastern region of the park, accessible via the John Muir Trail. All of the waterfalls are most impressive during May and June when the rivers are full with the spring runoff. In summer, on the other hand, the tributaries are almost dried up.

On the north side of the valley, El Capitan, the largest monolith on earth towers 4,785 feet. This granite giant, like the others *(Half Dome, North Dome, Three Brothers* and *Cathedral Rocks)* in the northern and eastern regions of Yosemite Valley are examples of the work done by the glaciers during the ice age. On the western side of El Capitan is the highest waterfall in the park. *Ribbon Falls* drops an impressive 1,612 feet to the valley below. From Yosemite Lodge, hiking trails lead over the northern flank of El Capitan (8 miles) to North Dome (7 1/2 miles) and to Eagle Peak (5 miles), the highest summit of the Three Brothers. A second trail to North Dome, only four miles in length, begins at Tioga Road east of Porcupine Flat. An overwhelming panorama of the entire Yosemite Valley is from the southern side of the valley at the 7,200 foot high *Glacier Point*. Judging from the masses of people who visit this area in the summer, it seems to be the most popular destination in the park. Glacier Point is also accessible by car. From Chinquapinoa, State Road 41, which leads to the southern entrance to the park, branches off into a 16 mile mountain road leading through beautiful landscapes. Hiking enthusiasts will prefer the Four Mile Trail or the footpath to the summit. From the summit, visitors will have an overview of all of this park's attractions. Over three thousand feet below is the tourist center of Yosemite Village, to the west the powerful El Capitan, directly opposite are the Yosemite Falls, the North Dome and the Tree Brothers and to the east are the Vernal and Nevada Waterfalls as well as the impressive Half Dome. In addition to this, a main attraction at Glacier Point is a sunset followed by a night with a full moon. The stars are so clear than it seems that they are almost within reach. A hiking trail leads through the beautiful landscape and up to the 8,800 foot high Half Dome which looks like a huge granite ball split vertically in the center. This hiking path does, however, require a good deal of effort. The trail begins at Happy Isles and is 7 1/2 miles long. Within the valley, an automobile is not necessary because a shuttle service operates frequently, taking visitors to all of the attractions.

Among the numerous tourists, many think that Yosemite Valley is the only attraction in this park. These people miss the three beautiful *Giant Sequoia Groves*. and the rugged alpine terrain. One can get an impression of this from a drive along *Tioga Road.* This road was originally built for the prospectors in 1882 and 1883. It was first improved and expanded in 1961. Along the road are beautiful, icy alpine lakes, blossoming meadows in summer, granite domes and lofty mountain peaks, which were covered by massive layers of ice 10,000 years ago.

Only a few miles west of the Tioga Pass entrance are the highest alpine meadows in the Sierra Nevada mountain range. The Tuolumne Meadows are a popular destination for many visitors in summer as a starting point for hikes through the rugged alpine region lasting several days. There are especially beautiful trails along the Tuolumne River, the second largest river in Yosemite National Park after the Merced River. The Tuolumne River flows through the Grand Canyon of the Tuolumne River in the north, which is only accessible on foot. A six mile long trail leads to the magnificent *Waterwheel Waterfall*. First, the hike is over a portion of the famous Pacific Crest Trail which transverses the park from north to south, then to Glen Aulin Campground on the Tuolumne River. After this, the path leads along the course of the river northwards to the waterfall. This marks the beginning of the rugged canyon which is over 5,000 feet in depth. At the northwestern end of this canyon, the construction of the *O'Shaughnessy Dam* has transformed the formerly picturesque Hetch Hetchy Valley into a huge reservoir which is the water supply for San Francisco. This reservoir is accessible from the Big Oak Flat entrance via the Hetch Hetchy Road. The Merced and Tuolumne Groves are two of the three sequoia groves in this national park. They are located in the Crane Flat Region only a few miles southeast of the Big Oak Flat entrance. Even more beautiful and more extensive as well is the *Mariposa Grove* near the southern entrance to the park. A road branches off of State Road 41 leading to a visitor centre with a large adjacent parking area. Private vehicles are not permitted past this point. For this reason, an open train operates from the end of April to the middle of November. The trip leads to the 250 acre grove and lasts around an hour. From June 4 to September 4, there are also daily tram tours between 9 am and 6 pm, departing every twenty minutes.

Prices: adults $5, seniors and children between 5 and 12 years of age $2.50.

The footpath is, however, more impressive, leading through 2½ miles of beautiful landscapes. The name Mariposa Grove, which means butterfly grove, somehow seems inappropriate to the gigantic trees. The largest among them is the Grizzly Giant, 210 feet tall with a circumference of almost 100 feet and a diameter of over 30 feet. Its age is estimated at 2,700 years.

Yosemite National Park / Practical Information

Accommodation

This national park is such a popular destination that in Yosemite Valley during the summer, one will be very lucky to find accommodation. Therefore, one should make reservations well in advance. This is especially true for the campgrounds located directly in the valley. For these, a reservation placed eight weeks in advance for the months from May to September. These are the campsites North Pines, Upper Pines, Upper River, Lower Pines, Lower River. Reservations are not accepted by telephone, but only in person at the National Park Service Campground Reservation Center or in writing by contacting Ticketron, Department R, 401 Hackensack Avenue, Hackensack, New Jersey 07601.

Camping sites, which do not require reservations are:

Backpackers Walk-In, in Yosemite Valley, 38 tent sites, $2 per person.

Sunnyside Walk-In, in Yosemite Valley, 25 tent sites, $2 per person.

Wawona, on Highway 41 in Wawona, 27 miles south of Yosemite Valley, 110 tent and RV sites, $6 per site.

Tamarack Flat, on Highway 120 east, 23 miles east of Yosemite Valley, 53 tent and RV sites, not well accessible for camping vehicles, $3 per site.

White Wolf, on Highway 120 east, 32 miles north of Yosemite Valley, 88 tent and RV sites, $6 per site.

Yosemite Creek, on Highway 120 east, 35 miles north of Yosemite Valley, 75 tent and RV sites, not well accessible for camping vehicles, $3 per site.

Porcupine Flat, on Highway 120 east, 38 miles north of Yosemite Valley, 55 tent and RV sites, only the front portion is accessible to camping vehicles, $3 per site.

Tenaya Lake Walk-In, on Highway 120 east, 46 miles northeast of Yosemite Valley, 50 tent sites, $6 per site.

Tuolumne Meadows, on Highway 120 east, 55 miles northeast of Yosemite Valley, 330 tent and RV sites, $9 per site.

Hotels/Motels: Ahwahnee Hotel, swimming pool, two tennis courts $150 to $160 for one and two persons, additional person $6, Tel: (209) 252-4848.

Curry Village, open April 1 to November 1, swimming pool, $45 to $65 for one and two persons, additional person $6, Tel: (209) 252-4848.

Curry Village Cabins, central bath, $35 to $50 for one and two persons.

Curry Village Tent Cabins, central bath, $24 for one and two persons, additional person $4.

Housekeeping Camp, central bath, small units for up to four persons, $25, open only in summer.

Wawona Hotel, open April 1 to November 30, swimming pool, tennis court, $65 for one and two persons, additional person $6, rooms without a bath $50, eight miles northwest of Mariposa Grove, Tel: (209) 252-4848.

White Wolf Lodge Tents, open only during the summer season, central bath, $24 for one and two persons, additional person $5.

Yosemite Lodge, open April 1 to November 1, swimming pool, $30 to $75 for one and two persons, additional person $8, Tel: (209) 252-4848.

Reservations can be made by contacting Tel: (209) 252-4848 or in writing to the following address: Yosemite Park and Curry Co. Reservations, 5410 East Home, Fresno, California 93727.

Bus Tours: Yosemite National Park has a total of 267 miles of well paved roadways. Therefore, it is possible to take long tours by bus, organised by the Tourist Center in Yosemite Village. For further information and possible reservations, one should go to the Ahwahnee Hotel, Camp Curry or the Yosemite Lodge. Tours last from two hours to an entire day. Information: (209) 372-1240.

Medical Care: In Yosemite Village, there is a small Medical Clinic, operated by the Samaritan Health Service.

General medicine, open from Monday to Friday from 9 am to 5:30 pm, Saturdays from 9 am to noon.

The clinic can be reached by telephone any time of day or night, Tel: (209) 372-4637.

Dental Care, open Monday to Friday from 8 am to 4:30 pm, Tel: (209) 372-4200.

The nearest hospital, depending on which region of the national park one happens to be, is in Merced, Fresno, Sonora, Bridgeport and Mariposa.

Restaurants: There are various restaurants in the national park where one can eat well. The largest selection is concentrated in Yosemite Valley. At the following restaurants, one should reserve a table in the evening:

The Ahwahnee Hotel, Tel: (209) 372-1489.

Tuolumne Meadows, Tel: (209) 372-1313.

White Wolf, Tel: (209) 372-1316.
Wawona Hotel, Tel: (209) 375-6556.

Sports

Cycling: Bicycles can be rented at the Yosemite Lodge and at the Curry Village Bike Stands for one hour or a full day.
Information: Tel: (209) 372-1208.

Hiking: The hiking trails in Yosemite National Park cover a total of 750 miles, and should entice every visitor to take off into the wilderness at least once on foot. Many of the attractions lie only a short hike away. Those who plan on taking longer hikes and spending the night in one of the wilderness camps will need a wilderness permit which is available in the visitor center in Yosemite Village or at the ranger station in Tuolumne Meadows free of charge.

Horseback Riding: There are four places within the national park with riding stables, which also offer interesting horseback tours: Yosemite Valley, Wawona, Whit Wolf, Tuolumne Meadows.
Information: Tel: (209) 372-1248.

Mountain Climbing: Yosemite National Park is a paradise for mountain climbers, offering all levels of difficulty. There are two mountain climbing schools in Yosemite Valley, one in Curry Village (Tel: (209) 372-1244) and one in Tuolumne Meadows (Tel: (209) 372-1335).

Swimming: Directly in Yosemite Village is a portion of the Merced River in which one can swim.

Visitor Center — Museums — Programmes

The Visitor Center in Yosemite Valley is open all year, in the summer from 8 am to 8 pm, and has an impressive photographic exhibition about the valley as well as a slide show and film presentation, Tel: (209) 372 4461. At the Visitor Center, there are a number of brochures and maps available. In addition, one can purchase books on Yosemite National Park. Other visitor centers are located in Mariposa Grove, at Glacier Point and in Tuolumne Meadows. These are only open during the tourist season and have information on the immediate regions. Directly near the Yosemite Visitor Center is the Indian Cultural Museum which presents the history of the Miwok and Paiute tribes. One should also be sure not to miss a visit to the museum in Mariposa Grove with information on the sequoiadendron. It is open from April to the middle of November from 8 am to 8 pm.

The ranger programme is especially extensive during the tourist season. Information is available in the park newspaper or is posted in the visitor centers and the ranger stations. Evening programmes take place during the entire year in the Valley Visitor Canter and in the Yosemite Lodge; in summer, there are also programmes at Glacier Point, Camp Curry and at the campsites Lower River, Lower Pines, Tuolumne Meadows, Crane Flat, Wawona, White Wolf and Bridalveil Creek. There are slide shows daily on Happy Isles during the summer. What is highly recommended are the tours guided by the rangers during the summer. These last from half an hour to a full day.

Important Addresses

National Park Address: Superintendent, P.O. Box 577, Yosemite National Park, California 95389, Tel: (209) 372-0200.

Informational Materials: Yosemite Natural History Association, Box 535, Yosemite National Park, California 95389, Tel: (209) 379-2646.

General Delivery: c/o General Delivery Main Post Office, Yosemite National Park, California 95389.

General Park Information: Tel: (209) 372-0264.

Weather and Road Conditions: Tel: (209) 372-4605.

Lost and Found: Lost and Found Office, P.O. Box 577 L, Yosemite, California 95389, Tel: (209) 372-4720. Open from Monday to Friday from 8 am to 4:30 pm.

Miscellaneous: The free park newspaper "The Yosemite Guide" with current programmes, special events and notices can be obtained in the visitor centres, ranger stations and at most of the entrances to the park.

Public laundry facilities and showers can be found in the Housekeeping Camp, located between Yosemite and Curry Village.

Youth Hostels →*Accommodation*